America's Other Muslims

Black Diasporic Worlds: Origins and Evolutions from New World Slaving

Series Editors: Antonio Tillis and Elizabeth West

Black Diasporic Worlds is a humanities series whose publications highlight the transnational Africana experience that has resulted from and/or emerged alongside European exploits in the Americas. Additionally, it encompasses contemporary and comparative contexts that are a byproduct of multidirectional shifting of Africana people over space and time. Further, the Black Diasporic Worlds series represents works that query the transcultural and transnational understandings of contemporary articulation and impact of "Africana" in Europe and other geographies outside of the Americas. Publications will look at African derived people/populations/cultures/civilizations resulting from the economic and political dynamics of new world slaving and the ways it has informed experiences, nationalistic and racial orientations, and shaped the Western world on both sides of the Atlantic. With regard to geographical scope, publications in this series will thus include works focusing on blacks in the Americas and in Europe, and could conceivably extend to the experiences of blacks beyond the Western world whose destinies have been shaped by the legacy or spillover of new world slaving.

Recent Titles

America's Other Muslims: Imam W.D. Mohammed, Islamic Reform, and the Making of American Islam, by Muhammad Fraser-Rahim
Afro-Asian Connections in Latin America and the Caribbean, edited by Luisa Marcela Ossa and Debbie Lee-DiStefano
Envisioning Black Feminist Voodoo Aesthetics: African Spirituality in American Cinema, by Kameelah L. Martin
Receptions of the Classics in the African Diaspora of the Hispanophone and Lusophone Worlds: Atlantis Otherwise, by Elisa Rizo and Madeleine M. Henry
Between Two Worlds: Jean Price-Mars, Haiti, and Africa, by Celucien L. Joseph, Jean Eddy Saint Paul, and Glodel Mezilas
African Modernity and the Philosophy of Culture in the Works of Femi Euba, by Iyunolu Osagie

America's Other Muslims

Imam W.D. Mohammed, Islamic Reform, and the Making of American Islam

Muhammad Fraser-Rahim

LEXINGTON BOOKS
Lanham • Boulder • New York • London

Published by Lexington Books
An imprint of The Rowman & Littlefield Publishing Group, Inc.
4501 Forbes Boulevard, Suite 200, Lanham, Maryland 20706
www.rowman.com

6 Tinworth Street, London SE11 5AL

Copyright © 2020 by The Rowman & Littlefield Publishing Group, Inc.

All rights reserved. No part of this book may be reproduced in any form or by any electronic or mechanical means, including information storage and retrieval systems, without written permission from the publisher, except by a reviewer who may quote passages in a review.

British Library Cataloguing in Publication Information Available

Library of Congress Cataloging-in-Publication Data

Library of Congress Control Number:2019956280
ISBN 978-1-4985-9019-8 (cloth)
ISBN 978-1-4985-9021-1 (pbk)
ISBN 978-1-4985-9020-4 (electronic)

For my parents and community,

who taught me *al Islam* of taste and its inner
and outer realities to remake the world

"Learn before you practice religion, as those who practice without learning usually become so fanatical that killing becomes an essential part of their behavior."

Hasan of Basra (642–728 CE)

Contents

Acknowledgments	ix
Preface	xi
Introduction	1
1 African American Islam in Context	7
2 Taffakur ("To Think, Ponder, Reflect"): Islam in West Africa and Islamic Revivalism	17
3 Africanizing Dixie: The Enslaved African Muslim Experience and the Black American Islamic Continuum	39
4 Imam W.D. Mohammed, the Patron Saint of American Islam: Personality, Intellectual Teachings, and Reformation	69
5 Walking with Brother Imam: The Community of W.D. Mohammed as a Counterweight to Extremism	91
Conclusion	103
Glossary of Terms	107
Bibliography	111
Index	127
About the Author	135

Acknowledgments

Numerous family members, friends, and colleagues have been instrumental in allowing my research and intellectual work to gain a footing in both academia and policy circles. Thank you Fatima and Yaya Fanusie, Kareem Sharif, Amir and Habeebah Muhammad, Mia Carey, Imam Luqman Rasheed, Imam Talib Shareef, Imam Earl El-Amin and Imam Benjamin Abdul Haqq, just to name a few. To my copyeditor, Sevim Kalyoncu, you were superb. I would also like to thank Laila Muhammad and the Muhammad estate for the use of W.D. Mohammed's speeches and writings throughout this book. The book is dedicated in memory of the Frasers and the Hamiltons, my maternal and paternal families, who have shaped my thinking and instilled in me a legacy of intellectual learning. Their experiences have included more than seven generations of college education and learning despite the difficulties and challenges of the African American experience. Their examples are the epitome of resilience, and for them I am eternally grateful.

Two academic scholars and mentors, Dr. Sulayman Nyang of Howard University and Dr. Alpha Bah of the College of Charleston, both of whom have passed, were influential in my intellectual and emotional growth as a student and trained me in understanding the intricacies of Africa, Islamic thought, and all things related to history, international relations, culture, and life. I am eternally indebted to them both. In addition, Shaykh Harun Rashid Faye, of the Zawiya of Moncks Corner, South Carolina, and of Senegal, West Africa, was extremely helpful in introducing me to in-depth knowledge of traditional Islamic sciences at a young age and served as a reliable teacher of understanding Islam through his lived experience and practice. Most important, I would like to show my appreciation to Herbert and Martha Fraser Abdur Rahim, my parents, who made the spiritual journey to awaken themselves and raise me and my siblings, Omar, Rabiah, Jamilah, and Aminah, in a utopian heaven in which they dedicated a lifetime of personal and community responsibility to help remake the world. Laila and Adam, savor the words and the history; this is for you.

I am also deeply thankful for the community that raised me in Charleston, South Carolina, which gave me my foundation. The red rice, the hoppins johns, the bean pies, the ginger punch, Walis Fish Supreme, Lateefs's, and that hot "fush" (fish) in my Gullah/Geechee vernacular sustained me and allowed me to be who I am now.

Masjid Al Jami Ar Rasheed was the "madrasa" in which my parents were my first Arabic teachers as well as the community that gave me love and attention. This community wasn't from overseas or distant places. It consisted of Americans—African Americans, Black Americans, descendants of enslaved Africans and white Americans alike, and in this village I learned the foundation of being me. I am eternally grateful! And finally, to Ms. Robinson (C. E. Williams Middle School), Bro. Nathaniel Razzaq, Bros. Hattie and Nabee Karim, Bro. Sadruddin El-Amin, Bro. Ernest, and the countless others from all over the world who have affected me, you all resonated with me more than you even know.

Preface

The historical links between religion, spirituality, and cultural identity on the continent of Africa and their journey to and development in the New World have been, in recent years, a source of increased discussion within academia and the diaspora of people of African descent. As a result of this growth in interest, the varying collective stories of the ethnic and religious descendants of Africa have been examined to understand how their origins in Africa have either been adapted, acculturated, or reformed into a new experience in new lands.[1]

Islam arrived in Africa in the eighth century after dispersing out of Arabia and spreading into modern-day North and West Africa. As such, the experiences of Islam in Africa established Islam's formative years on the continent via social agents of change in the form of traders and Sufi mystic interlocutors. The well-documented experiences of key Islamic personalities as well as Africa's rich Islamic heritage throughout the continent, specifically the Sahel region, detail a history of intellectual learning and scholarship in places like Timbuktu, Mali; Agade, Niger; and Kano, Nigeria.[2] These locations gathered together some of the brightest minds of their respective areas, and their research and classroom discussions centered around matters of astronomy, geometry, scientific inquiry, religious sciences, and treatises regarding their engagement with non-Muslim communities. These centers of learning present an alternative to the inaccurate but conventional wisdom that largely points to the Arab World / Middle East as the sole location of centers of learning for Islamic thought as well as its perceived ownership of philosophical, theological, and esoteric knowledge within Muslim communities.[3]

The aim of this book is to build on previous research addressing African Islamic heritage and provide a seminal work that links the Africana Islamic experience. Much of the literature and research on this topic limits the academic discourse in separate and non-aligned continuums, leaving much of the research to be divided into either African studies or African American studies. This often limits our ability to deeply examine the commonalities between the two areas of study.[4] Furthermore, there is also a tendency to relegate the Black American Islamic intellectual heritage to a category of *nouveau Islamique*, which seems impossible to enter into the traditional fields of Islamic studies or religion because of elements perceived as proto-Islamic by traditional perspectives, mostly Sunni and, oftentimes, Arab intellectuals.

This research strives to connect African Islam to African American Islam by looking at Islamic revivalism and making connections with the American Muslim revivalist, Imam Warith Deen Mohammed. By developing this approach, this study is one of the first to address the intersection between how American Muslim communities can be resilient against violent extremism in both a domestic and an overseas context as a result of the rise of transnational terrorist movements like the so-called Islamic State and al-Qa'ida who continue to gain appeal in Muslim populations globally. Furthermore, I also make the distinction and highlight the example of Imam W.D. Mohammed, an American-born Islamic preacher whose ancestry goes back to the sixteenth century forcible enslavement of West Africans who were brought to the Americas, where they sought to adapt, survive, and remain resilient in the face of bondage and persecution. The legacy of W.D. Mohammed, whose family members were the proverbial builders of American Islam, lies in his role in the evolution of millions of African Americans out of his father's race-centric theological and ideological teachings into universal Islamic values centered in the Black American cultural experience. In the experience of W.D. Mohammed and his community, we are given a compelling narrative and story to take lessons of good practices in the fight against violent extremism.

NOTES

1. Zain Abdullah, *Black Mecca: The African Muslims of Harlem* (New York: Oxford University Press, 2010).

2. Ousmane Kane, *Beyond Timbuktu: An Intellectual History of Muslim West Africa* (Cambridge, MA: Harvard University Press, 2016).

3. Edward E. Curtis IV, *The Call of Bilal: Islam in the African Diaspora* (Durham: University of North Carolina Press, 2014); Cheikh Hamidou Kane, *Ambiguous Adventures* (New York: Walker and Company, 1962).

4. Fallou Ngom, *Muslims beyond the Arab World: The Odyssey of Ajami and the Murriddiya* (New York: Oxford University Press, 2016).

Introduction

AFRICAN AMERICAN MUSLIMS IN CONTEXT

Black American Muslims represent one of the largest percentages of Muslims in America. Despite mainstream public narratives to the contrary, Muslims of African descent arrived in North America before the inception of the United States and have played an integral part in the development of American society. Developing from the enslaved African Muslim experience and journeying through Black Nationalism and heterodox and orthodox Islam, the expression of Islam's formative years in America are a direct reaction to American slavery, the Jim Crow laws, and the forced separation and breakdown of the black family. Emerging through organizations like the Ahmadiyya movement, the Moorish Science Temple, and the Nation of Islam, as well as individual Sunni, Shia, and Sufi practitioners, Islam in the Black American experience has taken shape on its own terms and through its own experiences and religious expression. This book explores how the Islamic continuum in the American experience developed into its own organic expression of independence and creativity while simultaneously preserving its time-honored religious tradition. Through the legacy of the American Muslim revivalist Imam W.D. Mohammed (1933–2008), we are given a philosophical, theological, and spiritual tradition that has carried out at least a forty-four-year counter-radicalization program and fostered a community of hundreds of thousands of adherents and sympathizers who are part of every fabric of American culture. This, in turn, has created a prototype for how communities can stay resilient against violent extremism domestically and globally. Equally important is the fact that, in researching, writing, and documenting the rich history of African American Muslims in public and private life, American public and global perceptions of Muslims in America in the nineteenth, twentieth, and twenty-first centuries were largely framed by an understanding of "Black" Islam. Through the well-publicized narratives of enslaved African Muslim personalities and key figures like boxing legend Muhammad Ali and numerous other musical and artistic performers, the idea of Islam being synonymous with the larger African American experience has been recognized.

However, in the era of 9/11 and its immediate aftermath there has been a gradual increase in activism by Arab, South Asian, and other ethnic Muslim communities who have ascended to positions of political and religious leadership. As a result of this increase in public engagement, as well as the large influxes of Muslims from non-European nation-states, these newly arrived Muslim immigrants, many of whom came as university students, physicians, and engineers, brought with them their own ideas, perceptions of the world, and vision of what Islam is or isn't. These viewpoints and perceptions were largely framed by where they lived, worked, and settled to achieve the American dream. Both Karen Brodkin, in her book *How Jews Became White Folks*, and David Roediger, in his book *The Wages of Whiteness*, capture this dialogue between who constitutes being an American and how the dream of American citizenship is achieved using race, political affiliation, social mobility, and economic power. Both books, in their own unique ways, address succinctly the impact race, religion, and notions of the "other" have in the context of Muslim communities as well. For many American Muslims of non-black ethnic origins, the achievement of the American dream has been rooted in their ability to pursue societal and cultural activities that connect them to broader notions of whiteness and affiliation with existing structures. Though not the scope of this book, this area of research must be explored further by future scholars of religion and Islam in particular. Two Muslim scholars, Atiya Husain and Moustafa Bayoumi, both discuss the categories of Muslim racialization, what impact they have on the current affairs of Muslim identity politics, and their role in public life. Husain in particular offers new research into how Muslim identity is perceived using categories historically rooted in the black/white debate and how popular perceptions equate Muslims with being foreign and brown as well as how these concepts and terms are evolving and require further inquiry. Husain's analysis, like those of other scholars studying Islamic thought in America, miss the opportunity to use only 9/11 as a point of gravity using simplistic and reductionist understanding of the state, empire, and US hegemony around the world.

For many Muslims (American or not), the Iraq wars and the broader conflict in the Middle East have been the predominant discourse around Muslim issues. Targeted killing, rectal rehydration, waterboarding, drone strikes, surveillance, the military industrial complex, and torture have been part of the litany of items around which Muslim solidarity issues have reached a consensus and have been part of the sermons from the pulpits of mosques on Fridays throughout the Islamic world. Despite these real and/or perceived grievances that occupy Muslim life throughout the world, there is not nor has there even been a consensus on the multitude of topics that are at the center of debate for Muslims. American Muslims in particular are no exception. Most recently, the topics of countering violent extremism, immigration, and the "Muslim ban" as part of the Trump administration public policy debate have been at the center of Muslim scholarly, activist, and religious community coffeehouse conversation. However, the question comes up, how are these seen, interpreted, or viewed in the diverse "Black" Muslim American communities. Is there a shared perspective in light of other issues that are at the forefront of African American communities regardless of religion, such as the subjects of drugs, gangs, and prison reform, which permeate African American life throughout the United States? As highlighted earlier, ranging from the first wave of immigrants from the Muslim world coming in the 1920s to the mid-1960s, to the second cohort of foreign-born Muslims arriving post-1965 along with "Black" Muslim convert communities, this convergence of ideas, ideological interpretations, and understandings of Islam has been part of this continuous evolution of an American Muslim community—but what cost has this cultural and religious milieu had? In most instances in the context of this book, "Black" Muslims have been erased from the public life of American Muslim activism, lobbying, and engagement despite their role as the foundational/indigenous American Muslim community.

OLD VERSUS NEW AMERICAN ISLAM

It is not the intention of this work to single out immigrant Muslim communities for contributing for the slow erasure of "Black" Islam in public life. It has been more than a decade since the death of the late Imam W.D. Mohammed, and the cultural and intellectual influence of the legacy of early African American Muslim communities is waning. In many instances, it is not just about the intersection between immigrant and African American Muslim communities but also the changing nature of how the American public views their Muslim neighbors, who were once known as both black and Muslim. Furthermore, the social media age we currently live in has created a new reactionary approach to politics, and the new wave of Muslims in political life has brought about a new type of Muslim identity, one which has different tones from the early African American Muslim community. The American Muslim community has seen demographic shifts, the emergence of suburban mosques, and the rise of mainstream Muslim institutions, such as the Islamic Society of North America and the Council of American Islamic Relations. Nevertheless, while internal bickering, losses of pioneer community members, and shifting views of Islamic thought and interpretation have contributed to a shift in the present-day internal and external dynamics of the African American Muslim community, there is still much to be gained from understanding the role of "Black" Muslim communities of the past and putting into context how the American Muslim community as a whole has come into existence.

Scholars such as Fatima Fanusie, Kambiz GhaneaBassiri, and Sally Howell provide some of the most authoritative bodies of analysis in looking critically at traditional notions of Islam, questions of modernity, and how American Muslims are perceived and view themselves in an ever-changing country and world. Howell writes, "The Muslim students who arrived in the 1950s and 1960s, most of them immigrant intellectuals from elite backgrounds who had little in common with the working-class Muslim Americans they met and worshipped with, were generally disparaging of the institutional practices they observed in Detroit as well. When they set about deconstructing American religious culture, capitalism and domestic politics in order to inspire a new Islamic awakening in their homelands, they found the example of established Muslim American communities useful only as a cautionary tale, as an example of what had gone wrong in the past and might go wrong again in the future." This interpretation is keenly important as American Muslims both in the contemporary context have wrestled through the ideas of what is legitimate Islam and how important it is to preserve culture, rituals and traditions of the past. Howell furthermore captures in her work, Gregory Starett who argues over the ideas of traditional, objectified and functional Islam in the context of American Muslims. Starett uses the term "functionalized" Islam to describe what would be considered modernist interpretive styles of Islam and "objectified Islam" building off of Eickelman and Piscatori who seek to show a shift from an earlier religious communal practice to one more focused on individualized textual interpretation. This shift for American Muslims, like other religious communities throughout America, radically has had a profound impact on how this research should be seen in the context of Islam in America and particularly Imam W.D. Mohammed and his revivalist practices and traditions offered in an American context. Furthermore, throughout this book, specific terminology is used to make a clear demarcation between some of the interpretive traditions of Islamic thought of the past, with centuries of transmission of knowledge in places throughout the Islamic world, including in Baghdad, Damascus, Cairo, and so on, and the "New World" traditions—Islam and its arrival into the West. In particular, the use of the term "African American Islam" over "Black Islam" is a purposeful attempt to move away from the pictorial account in describing the ethnic community of descendants of enslaved Africans using language that demonstrated their such evolution. C. Eric Lincoln and E. U. Essien-Udom, two prominent scholars of "Black Muslim" communities, use this term to describe the ideology, practices, and rituals of adherence to the Nation of Islam, but little scholarly research has focused on the shift and change of name, identity construction, and how practitioners perceive themselves. Many scholars of American Islam have adapted the use of the term "Blackamerican" or "Black Muslim" but I depart from this idea purposefully. I found this helpful and vitally important, as the book seeks to navigate through the space of W.D. Mohammed's approach, methodology, and framework in distinguishing his revivalist techniques inside an American context. W.D. Mohammed, more important, embraces this idea of independence in his desire to use language, terminology, and frameworks that connected him with the broader Muslim world, but also make a distinction of the unique circumstances, experiences, and engagement with Islam in an American context. For that, I make it a point to use the language of primary sources to explain this narrative and depart from some of these loose interpretations to describe descendants of enslaved Africans and their ancestral community of Imam W.D. Mohammed. This book more broadly explores the American Muslim Revivalist, Imam W.D. Mohammed—whom I characterize as the patron saint of American Islam—and his contribution to the intellectual, spiritual, and philosophical thought of African American Muslims in America. The research explores the intersection of the Africana experience and its encounter with race, religion, and Islamic reform. It also brings about the emergence of an American school of Islamic thought, created and established by the son of the leader of the former Nation of Islam who rejected his father's teachings and embraced normative Islam on his own terms. His interpretations of Islam were not only US American—they were also modern and responded to global trends in Islamic thought. His interpretations of Blackness were not only American but also diasporic and pan-African.

Chapter One

African American Islam in Context

SIGNIFICANCE OF THE STUDY

This book is built upon previous research on West African Islamic identity and its journey to America. It seeks to address the emergence of an American Islam that fuses together Islamic orthodoxy, Black Nationalism, spirituality, and American Protestantism along with elements from the continental West African Islamic revivalist tradition to create an emerging Black American Muslim community. This work is unique in that it is the first study on the American Muslim revivalist Imam W.D. Mohammed, and it demonstrates the continuum of the Islamic revivalist tradition that originated in West African Islamic institutions. It builds on the work of Dr. Fatima Fanusie, whose doctoral dissertation focused on Fard Muhammad, who was the ideological mastermind of the Nation of Islam and the intellectual teacher of Elijah Muhammad, the public leader of the Nation of Islam and father of the late Imam W.D. Mohammed.

Imam W.D. Mohammed (1933–2008) was a progressive African American Muslim leader, revivalist, theologian, and philosopher. His insights into the religious and cultural discourse of American, Islamic, and Black thought fuse together the historical linkages between Islamic intellectual contributions in West Africa and those of the larger Islamic world. His role in leading the largest conversion of American-born citizens to Islam and helping build the resulting community's legacy of being nonviolent, integrated members of American society serves as an example to minority communities throughout the world. Furthermore, it provides a window into a community that has undertaken a forty-two-year counter-radicalization program against extremism.

METHODOLOGICAL FRAMEWORK IN CONTEXT

This book seeks to fuse the intersection between normative Islam, Black American Islam, and the construction of various types of religious identities among Western-raised Muslims. It applies a sociocultural use of religion in its examination of the construction of group identity, scriptural interpretation, and W.D. Mohammed's Islamic revivalism based on the American experience. This vantage point provides the most optimal conceptual tool for not only understanding the formation of religious identity among Western-raised generations of Muslims but also delineating between the different types of identities acquired by Muslims living in the West.

Since the September 11, 2001, attacks on the World Trade Center and the Pentagon, social scientists have been focusing on identity construction among Western Muslims and have highlighted a number of factors that influence this process. Dr. Adis Duderija, in his seminal piece "Factors Determining Religious Identity Construction among Western-born Muslims: Towards a Theoretical Framework," provides a compelling analysis of the factors that directly affect the challenges facing Western-born Muslims in addressing religious identity, radicalization, Islamic reform, and integration into minority Muslim populations in the West.[1] Duderija builds on the research of Jocelyne Cesari who, in her book *When Islam and Democracy Meet: Muslims in Europe and the United States*, addresses similar issues of identity politics, integration, and assimilation in the Western context. Cesari provides an interesting analysis of key factors that affect Western Muslims broadly.

These factors include secularization and globalization; geopolitics and the nature of international environment; the broader socioeconomic, political, and legal contexts of "host societies"; and the diversity within the Muslim communities themselves, including ethnicity, family and socioeconomic background, and the length of immigration experience.[2] This book goes a step further than Dr. Cesari's work and outlines a theoretical framework that highlights how the sociocultural use of religious identity and the use of different scriptural interpretation models help construct as well as differentiate between different types of Western Muslim identity, with a particular focus on the community of W.D. Mohammed.

This work also addresses the impact of Imam W.D. Mohammed's teachings on a minority community in the West and how that community was able to integrate successfully into a non-Muslim-majority nation while simultaneously reconciling and channeling its nationalist, theological, and ideological teachings. The research was focused within the contemporary debate over Islam and its perceived proclivities toward violent actions, highlighting the example of Imam W.D. Mohammed, who led the largest mass conversion of American Muslims to a moderate form of Islam and galvanized a counter-radicalization movement in America that has continued for more than fifty years. Utilizing the First Amendment right to free speech, this movement has given rise to Muslim congressmen, doctors, lawyers, physicians, and war veterans as well as ordinary Muslim American citizens. Imam Mohammed's teachings, rooted in American values and democratic principles, reconcile religious tradition and country, thus serving as a prime example to Western Muslim communities who seek to address issues of identity, social cohesion, and coexistence. In particular, this work looks at African American and Black American Islam in three dimensions. The first dimension involves the emergence and cultivation of Islamic identity in West Africa followed its export into the New World. This transmission occurred via the first and second generations of enslaved Africans who brought a pacifist and nonviolent form of Islam into what would become the United States. Although many of these individuals may have, according to slaveholders' records, converted to Christianity, they may actually have hidden or appropriated certain religious identifications so as to preserve their identity and religious nature amid the difficult conditions of slave life in the American South. In fact, various provisions under certain mystical traditions in Islam, mainly Sufi orders in North and West Africa, facilitate and allow for practices to be hidden in order to protect the individual. All of this suggests that, in fact, the Arabic writings left by individuals such as Omar ibn Sayyid and Salih Bilali, two notable enslaved African Muslim personalities, provide insight into some of the specialized religious training that they may have received prior to coming in bondage to the Americas.

The second dimension includes the historical gap between African Islam and Black American Islam. It was during this period, from the early 1900s to the 1960s, that proto-Islamic movements, such as the Moorish Science Temple and the Nation of Islam, emerged. These movements addressed the unique social, cultural, and religious experiences that were deeply rooted in the enslaved African experience and built on the legacy of post-slavery, reconstruction, Jim Crow laws, and the civil rights movement.

The third dimension is the emergence of a specifically Western Islamic thought in America as a counterweight to violent extremism, in particular the spiritual, theological, and historical techniques utilized by W.D. Mohammed to develop and narrate an American form of Islam. Although W.D. Mohammed incorporated Islamic history into this uniquely American understanding of Islam, he departed from the rituals and traditions of the broader Islamic world. This served as a challenge to centuries-old traditions of Islamic learning. It can be argued that this independent thinking articulated by W.D. Mohammed and his adherents is a direct result of the experience of Black spirituality and Black religion as it emerged in the American environment. Thus, by offering a window into previous works on the topic while presenting new research in deconstructing W.D. Mohammed's lectures, books, religious intensive sessions, and travels, this work provides the intellectual framework for his contribution as an Islamic reformer in America and, ultimately, across the globe. It presents a two-phase process assessing the intellectual history of Imam W.D. Mohammed. The first phase addresses the literature of West African Islam, and the second analyzes the enslaved African Muslim experience in America. Through the examination of these two areas, a breadth of information that constitutes some of the foundational texts for this research is provided.

Scholarship on the topic of the late W.D. Mohammed as an Islamic thinker and teacher is still in its infancy. However, both Dr. Bruce Lawrence of Duke University and Dr. Timur Yuskaev of Hartford Seminary have provided chapters and research into W.D. Mohammed as an emergent thinker and a revivalist worthy of future study due to his unique commentary on Qur'anic exegesis. In his meticulous analysis of the Qur'an, Lawrence devotes an entire chapter to W.D. Mohammed largely as a result of the imam's fame and his courage to challenge Islamic scholars throughout the world for their inability to be flexible and accommodating or to modernize their thinking, thus resulting in a lack of progress. He argues that W.D. Mohammed's tenacity to boldly challenge old normative traditions of Islam, while at the same time staying true to his religious tenets, offers a positive example throughout the world.

Dr. Yuskaev offers an intimate account of W.D. Mohammed's spiritual and philosophical methodology by advocating that his religious style was through a spoken and living Qur'an. Yuskaev suggests that W.D. Mohammed's teachings are in the same religious tradition as past African American preachers, including Howard Thurman and Baptist preachers in the American South. Furthermore, he suggests that the traditions of W.D. Mohammed build on the legacy of the black church, American Protestantism, and the spiritual traditions of African traditional communities.[3] This compelling insight gives people a window into the thinking of W.D. Mohammed as an Islamic thinker and provides additional insights on African American and American cultural influences that shaped his teaching, which will be discussed further in this book.[4]

ENSLAVED AFRICAN MUSLIMS IN AMERICAN SOURCES

A steady but growing body of literature by social scientists has examined the Islamic identity of enslaved Africans brought to the New World. The stories captured by American newspapers, including runaway slave advertisements and even written accounts by slaveholders themselves, create a detailed narrative of Muslims of diverse religious experiences living in the Americas. Their stories present a narrative of enslaved Africans that describes their cultural, linguistic, and religious life and indicates a diversity of religious and spiritual understandings prior to conversion or assimilation into the religion of their slaveholders and the larger Christian society in the Americas.[5] Thomas Jefferson, for example, is known to have ordered a single translated copy of the Qur'an while studying at the College of William and Mary in 1765 in an effort to better understand religious identity and pluralism. Although Jefferson imagined a pluralistic United States, as reflected in his assistance in drafting the American Constitution, it is also documented that he owned African slaves. According to slave records, Jefferson's slaves had names such as Fatima, Fatimer, or Fatimatou, all of whom we can assume had their origin and familial roots in West Africa.[6]

To amplify this point even more, the now popularized written records of enslaved Africans, including Omar ibn Sayyid, Yarrow Mamout, Ibrahima Abdur Rahman, Nicholas Said, and Salih Bilali, indicate stories of enslaved Africans who were literate and had received training from religious men in intellectual centers of learning in the Sahel region of Africa.[7] Records indicate that all of these individuals were not only literate but also conversant in Islamic devotional practices. They also were known for their understanding of the Islamic spiritual practices of *tasawwuf* (Sufism) and were fluent in the Arabic language. Of all the autobiographies and biographies written by enslaved Africans or their immediate offspring, only Omar ibn Sayyid's autobiography was written in an African language. Sayyid's self-account was written entirely from memory using the Arabic script, and despite mistakes made by early translators of his story, Sayyid indicated he made a concerted effort to preserve his religious and spiritual origins. Furthermore, Yarrow Mamout from Georgetown, Washington, DC, and Salih Bilali from Sapelo Island, Georgia, were known to walk through their respective locations chanting Arabic words and were most likely Sufi devotional practitioners. Mamout's portrait was captured by the famous American painter Charles Wilson Peale in 1819 and was placed in the Philadelphia Museum.

Despite the existence of a Muslim presence in the Americas for more than a century, the history of this portion of the Muslim diaspora is gravely underresearched. There is evidence that Muslims had reached and interacted with Native American populations long before Columbus made the "New World" known to Europe. Nevertheless, it was Columbus's voyage and the resultant European onslaught that forever changed the history of Native Americans and Africans, including African Muslims. For 400 years, millions of Africans were forced into chattel slavery in the Americas and the Caribbean. The precise estimates of enslaved Africans of the Islamic faith vary greatly, but there is a consensus among scholars that there were Muslims all over the Americas, of whom roughly 20 to 40 percent were in the present-day United States.[8] Unfortunately, the resources related to these African Muslims are still filled with gaps. Over the past three decades, more research has been carried out and more has been written on the subject of enslaved Muslim Africans being brought to the Americas, and it is becoming an acknowledged phenomenon in the histories of many countries, including the United States. From Muslim-led rebellions in Brazil to Islamic scholars and enslaved princes held in bondage in South Carolina and Maryland, the history of how the West African arm of the Muslim *ummah* slowly bled is finally coming to light. The majority of citations represent scholarly research on this topic in English, Portuguese, French, Spanish, Italian, and German, but some are included in published primary resources in other languages as well, including Arabic. Incorporated sources were limited to those that focus on the topic or contain discreet chapters or sections on enslaved Muslims.[9] Much research remains to be done in this field of study, and there are likely additional documents still undiscovered that will bring further clarity into the life of these early Muslim communities. Such documents will likely include stories of women and children, but for now, these have yet to be discovered.

The work of Albert Raboteau in *Slave Religion: The "Invisible Institution"* and *African American Religion* provides intricate details of the spiritual experience of the enslaved African American community.[10] Raboteau places special emphasis on the type of Christianity encouraged and practiced on plantation locations across the American South while alluding to an African Muslim experience. He does not, however, provide a significant amount of detail in his description of this experience. In his work *The Slave Community*, John Blassingame also provides the context of the familial interactions and dietary habits as well as some of the spiritual practices of the enslaved African population.[11] Neither Blassingame nor Raboteau spend a significant amount of time informing the reader of the extent to which other religious practices were engaged, most importantly Islamic which left room for interpretation, curiosity and more research for scholars and researchers alike. Both scholars, bring incredible scholarship in understanding plantation life, but they both leave readers in suspense regarding other practices and beliefs, ultimately causing one to imagine certain Islamic religious practices being engaged on the plantations across the south and, hopefully, encouraging more research.

The works of C. Eric Lincoln and Lawrence Mamiya provide intersections of the enslaved African Muslim experience with the broader Black religion experience in America. Lincoln's seminal works, *The Black Muslims in America* and *The Black Church in the African American Experience,* seek to link the story of the enslaved African Muslim identity with that of the challenging conditions of life on the American plantation. They both also give a romanticized notion of an enslaved African Muslim experience through anecdotal stories, yet they do not quite give us a full picture of the number of enslaved African Muslims in America during the antebellum period or of their practices.

Finally, contemporary scholars such as Edward Curtis IV, Michael Gomez, Sherman Jackson, and Fatima Fanusie offer compelling insights into the intersection between the African Islam rooted in continental Africa and the development of new traditions of expression in the Americas, traditions that were built upon the enslaved African Muslim experience. Curtis offers examples of this intersection in his early books discussing the Nation of Islam as a social reform organization that addressed the conditions of early Black life in America. Gomez and Jackson provide perhaps the strongest research ever to be conducted on the development of new Islamic identities that offer competing legitimate religious alternatives to Islamic centers in the broader Muslim world. In his book *Islam and the Blackamerican: Looking toward a Third Resurrection,* Jackson seeks to look at life beyond the Arab world, focusing instead on the convergence of diverse Islamic communities and the creation of a new Islam that is both rooted in traditions of the past and willing to depart from them.[12] Neither Gomez nor Jackson necessarily offer a vision as to what these communities will look like in the future, nor are they advocates of the late W.D. Mohammed's rationale or thinking, as its ritual traditions differed slightly from those that are known and practiced throughout the broader Islamic world. At the same time, however, neither rejects W.D. Mohammed's teachings.[13]

ISLAM IN WEST AFRICA

In addition to the diaspora research conducted, scholars of West African Islam, including Leonardo A. Vilalon, Benjamin Soares, Cheikh Babou, Louis Brenner, Roman Loimier, and Ousmane Kane, offer a necessary connection to past research and scholarship in a historical context as well as a religious context that highlights the influence of Sufism. Rudolph Ware at the University of Michigan, in his work *The Walking Quran*, provides one of the most impressive contemporary written accounts of the origins of Islamic educational systems and the complexity of West African Islamic teachers' emphasis on passing down Islamic knowledge from generation to generation. Ware provides illustrative examples of how West African Islam, as a result of having spread downward from North Africa, shaped its roots according to its own cultural expression. He further highlights, like other researchers including Zachary Wright at Northwestern University, that the importance of Islamic identity, rooted in Islamic spirituality and fused with the African cultural reality, cultivated and gave rise to what we see as the West African Islamic expression. In his book *Living Knowledge in West African Islam*, Wright writes about the central role of Islamic revivalist thought in West African Islamic identity.[14] He carefully outlines the community of Ibrahim Niasse from Senegal as one example in a long line of West African Islamic teachers who emphasized a pragmatic, spiritual, and deeply religious form of Islamic practice.[15]

Ousmane Kane's new book, titled *Beyond Timbuktu: An Intellectual History of Muslim West Africa*, dives further into some of the intricacies highlighting the importance of Arabic literacy and how local African languages utilizing the Arabic script enriched Arabic as they adopted the language into their everyday life.[16] This version of Arabic became known as Ajami and is used for daily business transactions, recordkeeping, and religious purposes. When the nineteenth-century Senegalese religious leader Amadou Bamba Mbacke prescribed his adherents to write letters urging their countrymen to resist French colonial rule, he encouraged them to use Wolof, the language of Senegambia. When the Nigerian scholar and daughter of Muslim intellectual Usman Dan Fodio, Nana Asmau, composed a praise song of the Prophet Muhammad in the early 1800s, she did so in the Hausa language. Furthermore, when the eighteenth-century court poet Sayed Aidarusi honored his teacher with an adaptation of the Arabic epic "Umm al Qura," a famous Islamic and Arabic script, he wrote in Swahili, the language of fifty million East Africans. Yet, while all three wrote in their native languages, they used Ajami in their local language as a form of liberation that fused their cultural practices prior to Islam with the faith of their ancestors.[17]

As such, the experience of Islamic learning in West Africa provides a necessary insight into the emergence of African American Islam in the United States. Notable scholars including Zaid Abdullah of Temple University and Sulayman Nyang have argued that the gap between African Islam and African American Islam is the result of the American slave experience. The rituals, traditions, and knowledge transmissions were severed as communities and families were cut off from their traditional norms and value systems. Therefore, the emergence of the American encounter with Islam, separate from the West African experience, was largely a new Islamic expression that emerged in the early 1900s. It combined elements of mythology, Black nationalism, African spirituality, American Christianity, freemasonry, and revivalist thought from the Muslim world while seeking to create something unique to the Black American experience. Thus, the teachings of Imam W.D. Mohammed were in many ways a building block in understanding the origins of the enslaved African experience and West African Islam, but they were also a direct result of Islam's encounter with the circumstances of the American experience.[18]

NOTES

1. Adis Duderija, "Literature Review: Identity Construction in the Context of Being a Minority Immigrant Religion: The Case of Western-born Muslims," *Immigrants and Minorities* 25, no. 2 (2007).

2. Jocelyne Cesari, *When Islam and Democracy Meet: Muslims in Europe and the United States* (New York: Palgrave Macmillan, 2004).
3. C. Eric Lincoln, *Black Muslims in America*, 3rd ed. (Grand Rapids, MI: Eerdmans, 1994).
4. Clifton E. Marsh, *From Black Muslims to Muslims: The Transition from Separatism to Islam, 1930–1980* (Metuchen, NJ: Scarecrow Press, 1984).
5. Sylviane A. Diouf, *Servants of Allah: African Muslims Enslaved in the Americas*, 15th anniversary ed. (New York: New York University Press, 2013).
6. Allan D. Austin, *African Muslims in Antebellum America: Transatlantic Stories and Spiritual Struggles* (New York: Routledge, 1997).
7. Ibid.
8. Kambiz GhaneaBassiri, *A History of Islam in America: From the New World to the New World Order* (New York: Cambridge University Press, 2010).
9. Michael A. Gomez, *Pragmatism in the Age of Jihad: The Precolonial State of Bundu* (New York: Cambridge University Press, 1992).
10. Albert J. Raboteau, *Slave Religion: The "Invisible Institution" in the Antebellum South* (Oxford: Oxford University Press, 2004); Raboteau, *African American Religion* (Oxford: Oxford University Press, 1999).
11. John W. Blassingame, *The Slave Community: Plantation life in the Antebellum South* (Oxford: Oxford University Press, 1979).
12. Sherman A. Jackson, *Islam and the Blackamerican: Looking toward the Third Resurrection* (Oxford: Oxford University Press, 2011).
13. Louis Lomax, *When the Word Is Given* (Westport, CT: Greenwood Press, 1963).
14. Zachary V. Wright, *Living Knowledge in West African Islam: The Sufi Community of Ibrahim Niasse* (Leiden: Brill, 2015).
15. Cheikh Anta Babou, *Fighting the Greater Jihad: Amadu Bamba and the Founding of the Muridiyya of Senegal, 1852–1913* (Athens: Ohio University Press, 2007).
16. Ousmane Oumar Kane, *Beyond Timbuktu: An Intellectual History of Muslim West Africa* (Camrbidge, MA: Harvard University Press, 2016).
17. Ibid.
18. Ibid.

Chapter Two

Taffakur ("To Think, Ponder, Reflect")

Islam in West Africa and Islamic Revivalism

ISLAM'S ORIGINS

Islam is a monotheistic religion that shares its origins and values with the other Abrahamic faiths of Judaism and Christianity. It originated in the present-day Middle East and quickly became one of the three great world religions. The vast desert region of the Arabian Peninsula and modern-day Saudi Arabia was the birthplace of Muhammad, the founder of the formalized religion of Islam. Born in Mecca in 570 AD, Muhammad emerged out of humble beginnings; he was orphaned at a young age and raised by numerous family members throughout his childhood. Around the age of 40, he was divinely tapped to become the Prophet of Islam. Hence, he abolished idolatry, established and promoted the oneness of God, and eradicated numerous social and moral dysfunctional traits that had permeated the Arabian society. The death of Muhammad in 632 AD gave rise to a new beginning for the Islamic community.[1] The death of the leader of Islam would give rise to four *caliphs* or rulers: Abu Bakr (632–634 AD), Umar (634–644 AD), Uthman (644–656 AD), and Ali (656–661 AD). During the reigns of these caliphs, Islam expanded into new frontiers beyond the Arab world, going east toward Asia and west into Africa.[2]

BILAL, RACE, AND THE EARLY MUSLIM COMPANIONS

Before elaborating on how Islam spread into West Africa, it is important to note that the Qur'an, Islam's holy text, expresses no racial or color prejudice in explicit terms. In the following passages, it speaks directly to the importance of diversity and the lack of superiority of one ethnic group over another:

> Among God's signs are the creation of the heavens and of the earth and the diversity of your languages and of your colors. In this indeed are the signs for those who know. (Surah Rum, 30:22)[3]
> O People! We have created you from a male and a female and we have made you into nations and tribes so that you may come to know one another. The noblest among you in the eyes of God is the most righteous/pious, for God is knowing and well informed. (Surah Hujarat, 49:13)[4]

However, despite this egalitarian ideal, in Muslim tradition, as in other religious traditions, the issue of discrimination certainly is something that existed and had to be addressed. Muhammad's last sermon further amplifies the points addressed in the surahs above and admonishes the continued issue of a predominance of Arab superiority among the early Muslim community. This quotation from Muhammad's Farewell Sermon is rather more specific:

> All mankind is from Adam, and an Arab has no superiority over a non-Arab nor does a non-Arab have any superiority over an Arab; also a white has no superiority over a black nor does a black have any superiority over a white, except by piety and good action.
> Learn that every Muslim is a brother to every Muslim and that the Muslims constitute one brotherhood. Nothing shall be legitimate to a Muslim which belongs to a fellow Muslim unless it was given freely and willingly. Do not, therefore, do injustice to yourselves.
> Remember, one day you will appear before Allah and answer for your deeds. So beware, do not sway from the path of righteousness after I am gone.[5]

And finally, Arnold J. Toynbee fuses his personal and documented accounts in this famous passage from his book *A Study of History*:

> For instance, the Primitive Arabs who were the ruling element in the Umayyad Caliphate called themselves "the swarthy people," with a connotation of racial superiority, and their Persian and Turkish subjects "the ruddy people," with a connotation of racial inferiority: this is to say, they drew the same distinction that we draw between blondes and brunettes but reversed the values which we assign to the two shades of white. Gentleman may prefer blondes; but brunettes are the first choice of Allah's "Chosen people." Moreover, the Arabs and all other White Muslims, whether brunettes or blondes, have always been free from colour-prejudice *vis-à-vis* the non-White races; and, at the present day, Muslims still make that dichotomy of the human family which Western Christians used to make in the Middle Ages. They divide Mankind into Believers and Unbelievers who are all potentially Believers; and this division cuts across every difference of Physical Race. This liberality is more remarkable in White Muslims today than it was in the White Western Christians in our Middle

Ages; for our medieval forefathers had little or no contact with peoples of a different color, whereas the White Muslims were in contact with the Negroes of Africa and with the dark-skinned peoples of India from the beginning and have increased that contact steadily, until nowadays White and Blacks are intermingled, under the aegis of Islam, throughout the length and breadth of the Indian and the African Continent. Under this searching test, the White Muslims have demonstrated their freedom and race-feeling by the most convincing of all proofs: they have given their daughters to black Muslims in marriage.[6]

This is important to highlight as we seek to further explore the intersectionality between how Islam spread into West Africa and the rest of the globe. Islam's origins do have foundational roots in the Arab world just like those of its Judeo-Christian cousins, and a large segment of its early adherents were in fact Arab; however, from the beginning of Islam, its most faithful early converts were of diverse backgrounds, including African ancestry. Though there were a number of black companions of Muhammad, including Usamah bin Zayd, Sa'ad Al Aswad As Sulami, Ammar bin Yasir, and Mihja bin Salih; the most notable of all is Bilal Ibn Rabah. Bilal's role as an integral member of the early Islamic faith would serve as a vital source of inspiration for Black Muslims globally and would play an almost iconoclastic role in the Black American Muslim community as it emerged in the early 1900s. Bilal was an enslaved African belonging to Umayyah ibn Khalaf who was of Arab ancestry. He was one of many enslaved Africans from Abyssinia (present-day Ethiopia). Bilal is considered the first caller to prayer, or *Muezzin,* and he was the seventh person to embrace Islam during the formative early years of Islam as a religion. Having been among the earliest followers of Muhammad, Bilal is considered to have been one who suffered from some of the most difficult racial, ethnic, and religious persecution by the dominant opposition tribe within the early Islamic community, the Quraysh. Abu Bakr, a close companion of Muhammad, was largely protected from torture and hostilities because of his tribal affiliation.

The wrath of those who rejected the normative religious practices in the Arabian Peninsula fell upon the Muslims who had no tribe to defend them. Umayyah ibn Khalaf would force Bilal to go outside during the hottest part of the day wearing a heavy suit of armor, where he would then be thrown face down in the sand and left to bake in the sun. He would not return except to turn him on his back. According to historical Islamic and Arabic sources, he would have a gigantic rock placed on Bilal's chest and then Ibn Khalaf would say, "You will stay here until you die or deny Muhammad and worship al-Lat and al-'Uzzah."[7] Bilal is said to have reacted only by saying, "One, One." Bilal's endurance during the early days of the Muslim community has remained a critical and important symbolism within both the historical and the contemporary Islamic community and, more important, within

Black Muslim communities worldwide. Bilal contributed to the early Muslim community by helping to establish the formal call to prayer.

When Muhammad was commissioned with the role of prophet in his fortieth year, prayer was the first instruction given by divine command. According to primary Arabic sources, the archangel Jibril (Gabriel) showed Muhammad how to perform the ablution from a spring before performing the ritual Islamic prayer.[8] Muhammad then showed his wife, Khadijah, how to perform the prayer, thus making her the first person to engage in the ritual tradition. After this event, Muhammad began to pray two cycles of ritual prayer twice a day, once in the morning and again in the evening. In the ninth year of his mission as the prophet of Islam, the archangel Jibril took Muhammad on a journey to Jerusalem, where the archangel gave guidance on a fixed amount of prayer times, which then became established by the Muslim community for future generations to come.

These stories are integral within the Islamic tradition because of the establishment of the tradition of calling the Islamic prayer. This is the basis of regulation for Muslims who gather at the appointed times—early morning, midday, midafternoon, dusk, and after sundown—to perform the *salat*, the Muslim prayer that includes the prostration of the body in the direction of Mecca. We will see later in chapter 4 how W.D. Mohammed uses the memory of Bilal as a form of agency, identity, and spiritual affirmation to connect Black American Islam with the Islamic religion and the recovery of black dignity, pride, and power.

BLACK PRESENCE AMONG EARLY MUSLIM ADHERENTS

The introduction of Islam created an entirely new situation in terms of race as a social construct. In particular, its terminology presents challenges, for terms of color applied to individuals in the early Islamic period are quite ambiguous in primary Arabic source documents. Specifically, the adjective "black" (*aswad*) applies both to Africans and to collective groups of Europeans who are considered Caucasians. This means that a person labeled as "black" need not be of African descent; however, we will work under the assumption that the term for "blacks" refers to Africans. Throughout the research presented we maintain the terminology of the original Arabic sources when referring to those labeled as black (*aswad*, pl. *Sudan*), Ethiopians (*Habashi*, pl. *Ahbash*), or Africans (*Zanj*, pl. *Zunuj*).[9]

As such, all of the ancient civilizations of the Middle East and Asia were relatively local and regional in terms of their focus and early interactions, making them largely homogenous in terms of ethnic makeup. The Roman Empire, even though vast and wide in its reach, was largely Mediterranean in its orientation and as a society at large. However, Islam, as a new religion bringing in converts, demonstrated a universal society with a plethora of racial mixes, extending to Europe, Africa, and the Far East. I argue that in the case of pre-Islamic and early Islamic poetry as well as the society at large, there seem to be mixed attitudes toward those who have African ancestry. This had implications for the later periods in Islam's early foundational years, and as the Islamic world expanded into new frontiers, it created problems in the sentiment, attitudes, and preoccupations of individuals and nation-states. The references to black people in pre-Islamic Arabian society largely allude to Ethiopians—commonly called *Habash*, an Arabic name from which the word *Abyssinian* is derived. As such, there is a plethora of evidence to show an anti-black prejudice within the poems of the early Arabian society. One such poem laments:

> If my color were pink, women would love me,
> but the lord has marred me with blackness[10]

In another poem of the time, attributed to poets of African ancestry, there seems to be a consistent attitude of the poets who were conscious of their birth and endured considerable insults. Nusayb ibn Rabah, a gifted poet of the classical period, writes:

> Blackness does not diminish me, as long as I have this tongue and this stout heart. Some are raised up by means of their lineage the verses of my poems are my lineage! How much better a keen-minded, clear spoken black than a mute white![11]

Equally important, there were a few books in defense of those of African ancestry in the early period of Islamic history and the proceeding generations, but they were usually directed toward those of Ethiopian heritage. One of the earliest treatises on this subject was written by Jamal al-Din Abu'l Faraj ibn al Jawzi, titled *The Likening of the Darkness of the Merits of the Blacks and the Ethiopians*. This book seeks to defend those of African ancestry and the accusations made against the community. In one passage it states:

> I have seen a number of outstanding Ethiopians whose hearts were breaking because of their black color. So I let them know that respect is based on the performance of good deeds, and not on beautiful forms. I therefore composed for them this book, which deals with a good number of Ethiopians and Blacks.[12]

A second work, *The Raising of the Status of the Ethiopians*, based on the previous work by al-Jawzi, was completed by the famous Egyptian Islamic scholar Jalal al Din al Suyuti. Al Suyuti also wrote a similar text, *The Colored Brocade on the Good Qualities of Ethiopians*.

These historical accounts, documented in primary and secondary sources throughout the early Islamic period and ultimately the broader Arab world, suggest a pattern of racial superiority over African identity oftentimes masqueraded as the desire of attaining whiteness by Arab communities. However, simple constructs to deduce these ideas over races as black and white or abstract aren't important either. Conventional wisdom in many Islamic institutions in the known Arab Muslim world often place Islam in the category of Arab equaling whiteness, masculine, public, and the embodiment of orthodoxy, while African traditional practices and their subsequent conversion in Black Africa is equated with being heavily spiritually possessed, African, feminine, and oral. Neither of these examples accurately portrays these ideas quite well, and more nuanced attention is required to unpack centuries-old themes.[13] These examples and illustrations serve as important building blocks as we think more broadly about the expansion of Islam into West Africa as well as the limitations that Islamic scholars faced as a result of real and perceived racial prejudices.[14]

ISLAM IN WEST AFRICA

West Africa's first contact with Islam came in the eighth century, during the development of the trans-Saharan trade routes that spread southward from North Africa to West Africa.[15] Immediately after the Arabs began to dominate North Africa, the powerful Umayyad force sought to organize military units and slave raids into the Southern part of Morocco and the powerful Ghanaian civilization. These highly organized expeditions were extremely profitable in obtaining physical manpower and massive amounts of gold supplies. The traders of the East were also influential in spreading the faith of Islam as commercial interactions with the West African coast provided an invested interest in spreading the faith of Islam. Religious reform movements also encouraged this spread. The Almoravid movement, for example, which began with the Sanhaja ethnic group in the Sahara, was established by Abdullah ibn Yasin, an eleventh-century theologian and proselytizer of Islam who sought to bring about purity to the unorthodox practices that were creeping into the Islamic community. In fact, one might argue that his views were the first cycle in an effort by Islamic preachers to bring fundamental basic teachings to the region and model it after the first community created by Prophet Muhammad and his successors.[16] Another religious reformer, Abdullah Muhammad ibn Tifat, was the first in a long line of reformers who would seek to expand their doctrine east and south into the heart of traditional Black Africa.

As Islam reached the Savannah regions and made major inroads into West Africa, a wealth of documents were compiled that provide accurate perspectives of the life, rituals, and traditions of West African society. Muslim historians and geographers today are able to present illustrative accounts and written records of Muslim rulers and people living in West Africa, including Al Khwarzimi, Ibn Munabbah, Al-Masudi, Al Bakri, Abul Fida, Ibn Battuta, Ibn Khaldun, Ibn Dadlallah al-Umari, Mahmud al Kati, Ibn al Mukhtar, and Abd al Rahman al Sa'di.[17] As Islam continued to spread outward from the Savannah regions in West Africa, trade and commercial exchange paved the way for the introduction of new elements into the development of Islam in West Africa, including literacy and religious learning. The written history and artifacts of the most well-known empires of the classical period of Islam in West Africa, Ghana, Mali, Songhay, and Kanem Bornu (located in present-day Nigeria and the Lake Chad Basin), provide insights into the robust intellectual legacy of these societies as they emerged and transitioned into Islamic centers of learning. The texts *Tarikh al Sudan* (*The History of the Sudan*) by Al-Sadi and *Tarikh al-Fattash* by Muhammad al-Kati are well-known historical documents that provide further insights. As Rudolph T. Ware notes in *The Walking Qur'an*, "Armed with reed pens, wooden slate boards, and the Book they carried within their own bodies (i.e., the memorized Qur'an), clerics (i.e., ulama or marabouts) brought Islam to sub-Saharan West Africa."[18]

As recorded in his *Rihla*, the fourteenth-century traveler Ibn Battuta also passed through Timbuktu in 1353 and noted the great importance placed on Islamic learning in Mali, especially the memorization of the Qur'an. Timbuktu was an epicenter of highly acclaimed and reputable establishments for Islamic learning and commercial activity. It was home to Sankore University, Jingaray Ber University, and Sidi Yaya University, as well as around 200 Qur'anic religious schools.[19] Mali also is critically important to this research as we begin to make the connections between West African history and the spread of Islam to America. Of the four normative Sunni legal schools, or *madhab*, the Maliki madhab was the dominant interpretive tradition of West Africa, having been inherited largely from Islam coming from North Africa, as in the cases of the Maghreb and the Iberian Peninsula. In the 15th and 16th centuries, West African cities such as Timbuktu, Mali; Zinder, Niger; and Kano, Nigeria, emerged as thriving centers of Islamic thought, providing instruction in Arabic, Islamic spirituality (Sufism), Qur'anic exegesis, and Islamic law. Like Catholic institutions in Europe, early Muslim institutions followed a quadrivium-style education focusing on a holistic approach to learning that combined the public and religious realms in a way that encouraged balance in one's life. Furthermore, in both those religious centers of learning and private circles of learning in West Africa, a widely religious text known as the *Risala*, written by the Tunisian scholar Ibn Abi Zayd al Qayrawani, provided Islamic religious and spiritual science in practical terms.

The Islamic faith in Sub-Saharan Africa developed through the process of learned, scholarly, and spiritually pious men. Central to the expansion of Islam in Western Africa and the beginning of Islamization was the emphasis on Islamic education. Ibn Battuta wrote the following about the people of Mali a century after the creation of Sankore University:

> They are very zealous in their attempts to learn the holy Qur'an by heart. In the event that their children are negligent in this respect, fetters are placed on the children's feet and are left until the children can recite the Qur'an from memory. On a holiday, I went to see the hudge, and seeing his children in chains, I asked him, "Aren't you going to let them go?" He answered, "I won't let them go until they know the Qur'an by heart." Another day I passed a young Negro with a handsome face who was wearing superb (clothes) . . . and carrying a heavy chain around his feet. I asked the person who was with me, "What did that boy do? Did he murder someone?" The young Negro heard my question and began to laugh. My colleague told me, "He has been chained up only to force him to commit the Qur'an to memory."[20]

An important epistemological approach that was and continues to be central to West Africans' understanding of Islam is the memorization of the Qur'an. Like Islamic scholarship in the Arab Middle East, Islamic studies in West Africa started at the Qur'anic school where young pupils would begin to learn the Qur'an as young as four and were taught to memorize the Qur'an and the Arabic script. Some students in traditional West African Islamic schools, including those who were Arabs or foreign exchange students from North Africa, were not actually able to understand the meaning of or read the Qur'an, but they were conversant in Qur'anic Arabic and had mastery of Islamic sciences as well as a number of other subjects by the time they completed their studies.

In addition to providing the formal process of religious learning, including at Sankore University in Timbuktu, which also served as a mosque and an intellectual center on a wealth of Islamic topics, West Africa competed with other centers of higher learning in neighboring North Africa. There was no single unified curriculum in West Africa, but certain common texts were used by North African and West African scholars alike.[21] In Timbuktu, literacy and books transcended scholarly value and symbolized wealth, power, and *Baraka* (blessings) in addition to serving as an effective means of transmitting key information.[22] One such example was based on the model established by religious scholars of Timbuktu. In this educational and religious setting, an old method of teaching was adopted by the founder of the Maliki School of Islamic thought, Imam Malik Ibn Anas, a notable scholar of Sunni Islam and one of the leading four imams in Sunni Islamic jurisprudence. In this teaching method, a student reads before the teacher and the teacher reads back to the student. If the student makes a mistake, the teacher corrects him.

The teacher then interprets and explains sacred texts to the student. As part of this student/teacher relationship, the following texts were well known and popular in this time period and are still utilized among West African Islamic institutions in the modern era:[23]

1. *Qawa'id as-Salah* is a treatise of about thirty pages that discusses the principles of Islamic prayer and articles of faith according to the Islamic tradition.
2. *Mukhtasar al-Akhdari*, by Abu Zaid Abdur Rahman al-Akhaari, is an introduction to Islamic jurisprudence (*fiqh*) with emphasis on purification of the heart and Islamic spirituality (*tasawwuf*/Sufism), ritual purity (*tahara*), and prayer (*salah*).
3. *Al-Ashmawiyyah*, by Abd al Bari al Ashmawi ar Rifai, is an introductory text that covers ritual purity (*taharah*), prayer (*salah*), and fasting (*sawm*). It is studied alongside:
4. *Manzumah al Qurtubi fil-Ibadat*, by Yahya al-Qurtubi, is an introductory text covering the five pillars of Islam: doctrinal belief/creed (*aqidah*), prayer (*salah*), fasting (*sawm*), alms (*zakah*), and pilgrimage to Islam's holy sites in Mecca, Saudi Arabia (*hajj*).
5. *Al Muqaddimah al Izziyah*, by Abu Hassan Ali ash Shadili, is seen as an intermediate text that concerns the jurisprudence of Islamic worship.[24]
6. *Nazmu Muqaddimah Ibn Rushd*, by Abd ar Rahman ar Rafai, is an intermediate text that builds on the works of *Manzumah al Qurtubi*. It goes into detail about the five pillars of Islam and the legal opinions associated with each.
7. *Al Risalah*, by Abu Muhammada Abdullah ibn Abi Zayd al Qayrawani, is another intermediate text associated with the early curriculum in Islamic traditional schooling in West Africa and Timbuktu. The first half is on Islamic worship, with emphasis on Islamic jurisprudence concerning marriage, divorce, commercial transactions, inheritance, punishment laws, and spirituality. This text is unique in that it is infused with examples of traditions of the Prophet Muhammad, and it has been continuously taught for centuries.
8. *Al Murshid al Mu'in*, by Ibn Ashir, is a comprehensive body of work that is categorized into three Islamic sciences: Ashari Islamic theology, Maliki jurisprudence, and Islamic spirituality based on the practices of the Sufi mystic Imam Junaid al-Baghdadi.
9. *Misbah al Salik*, by Abd al Wasif Muhammad, is one of the first advanced books that is studied as an entry point into more advanced theological works in the Maliki school of thought. This book details issues of theology, Islamic jurisprudence (i.e., worship, marriage, commercial transactions, judicial, etc.), and social ethics.

Besides the above-mentioned texts, there are other Maliki and general Islamic classical textbooks used in West Africa, but this list provides a content analysis of just some of the more popular and well-known religious textbooks. In addition, throughout West Africa is a text known as *Al Ajrumiyah*. In many, if not all, of the West African Islamic centers of learning, this thirteenth-century book of Arabic grammar is used as the foundational text for beginning to develop an understanding of classical Arabic education.[25] Building from the larger Arab world, this text, along with *Alfiya*, is one of the first books memorized after the Qur'an. *Alfiya* is a rhymed written Arabic grammarian book composed in the thirteenth century that was used throughout Islamic religious institutions in West and North Africa. Having combed through both *Al Ajrumiya* with *Alfiya*, West African Muslims were equipped with highly skilled Arabic language instruction that would serve both religious and commercial purposes for a lifetime. This is an important feature as we expound later into details about the importance of Arabic literacy in West Africa and how West African Islamic revivalists used language as a form of resistance and a means to enrichment for their communities.

Through the gradual process of Islam's expansion into West Africa, the Islamic faith was hugely impacted through the influence of localizing and culturally adapting into the traditional and local customs of the various nation-states. Traditions prior to the advent of Islam had largely been in the form of African traditional religion. After the introduction of Islam, West Africans were able to articulate a sense of amalgamation of their traditional beliefs and practices. Local Muslim leaders were able to fuse together Arabic literacy and their knowledge of pre- and post- Islamic mystical traditions to bring in new converts; empower *marabouts*, local religious chiefs; and incorporate the use of Qur'anic verses, which came to replace previous indigenous talismans and medicinal packets, for protections. These amulets replaced previous African traditional artifacts with highly complex Arabic Islamic formulas. This practice of syncretism has been a common practice in the Islamization process throughout the world for centuries.[26] Diane Simpson, Asim Roy, Richard Bengal, Clifford Geertz, and Fatima Fanusie argue that this strategy was an effective tool of Islamization that utilized song, stories, and rituals to inculcate, in this case, Islam as a normative tradition in local West African society.[27] David Robinson, a West African scholar of Islam, furthers this perspective in the following passage: "There is nothing pejorative about the Africanization of Islam. . . . There is something pejorative about the way that European and many Mediterranean-based Muslims have perceived African Islam and the Africanization of Islam."[28]

In addition, Ware furthers this analysis by highlighting the dichotomy of African Islamic religious institutions that are faced with both the private and public of negotiating between a narrative of adoption and adaptation within the religious sphere.[29]

TASAWWUF

To understand the role of West African Islam, one must also understand the dynamic and the importance of Islamic spirituality, in this case *tasawwuf*, or Sufism,[30] in the local context. Many historians and specialists on Sufism point out that the term "tasawwuf" etymologically derives from the term "*suf*" or "wool," in reference to the coarse woolen garment worn by the early ascetic practitioners of this mystical path. Universal among Islamic spiritualists are the calls for *zuhd* (asceticism), *wara* (sincerity), and *rila* (acceptance of the divine decree of individuals). The Sufi belief is that reason alone is not sufficient to make decisions; therefore, it is essential to understand the external and the hidden realities of both the spiritual and physical realms. To fully understand these realities, one must undergo physical and spiritual training that require an enlightened religious and spiritual guide who is trained in Islamic sciences. Individuals undergoing such training eventually came to be labeled/named as Muslim mystics, or Sufis, and the outfits worn by early practitioners were a sign of austerity, purity, and a renunciation of the worldly life, a common theme articulated in many of the mystical paths throughout the Islamic world. For al-Qushayri, the eleventh-century Persian mystic, the term "Sufi" applied to groups of men united by their common desire toward a path of *zuhd*, defined as a renunciation of items not important in the spiritual and religious life. In the attempt to distinguish themselves from their Muslim coreligionists, early Sufis, including Al Jundayd of the ninth century, defined tasawwuf as the following:

> It is to render the heart independent of other creatures by purifying it, ridding oneself of natural instincts, extinguishing one's purely human qualities, avoiding the activities of one's natural instincts, and to acquire spiritual qualities, imbuing oneself with gnostic knowledge, giving preference to that which has eternal priority, giving good counsel to all members of the [Muslim] community, being entirely faithful to God and following the messenger in conformity with the *sharia*.[31]

These doctrinal beliefs by adherents to Sufism provide an important insight into how West Africans ultimately came to use their spiritual practices to aid them in everyday life. Some of the foremost experts of Sufism in the West today are Dr. Carl Ernst, Dr. William Chittick, and Dr. Syed Hussein Nasr. These individuals not only provide compelling insights into the future of Sufism as a study but also give us insights into the historical perspectives of Sufism. In the book *Sufi Martyrs of Love*, Carl Ernst and Bruce Lawrence provide details of how to interpret Sufi orders beyond old normative traditions:

> Our thesis is that a Sufi order . . . is more than parasitical legitimization of power or a nostalgic reverence for bygone saints; it is instead a complex of spiritual practice, historical memory and ethical models, which continues to evolve from its medieval Islamic origins in response to the political, ideological and technological transformations of the contemporary world.[32]

Using a number of primary sources, Ernst and Lawrence give us insight into the Christi Sufi order residing in Southeast Asia and describe their analysis on the basis of a historical Sufi tradition of idioms, saints, and those who link themselves with a chain of spiritual wise men and their centuries-old traditions. However, the roles of rank-and-file or otherwise "ordinary" followers seem rather vague in early Chishtiyya traditions. What unfolds, according to Rudiger Seesemann, is a living Sufi tradition, compared to the orientalist narrative of an inevitable decline in what is seen as non-normative or mainstream folk Islam. As Seesemann argues, this creates a living spiritual experience "embedded in and reenacted by historical memory, and a cyclical revival of Sufi teachings culminating in its latest transformation to 'cyber Sufism,'" and this is part of a revival of the Sufi Islamic traditions to facilitate the direct involvement of followers in a lived and experiential spiritual experience.[33]

The vital contributions of early Sufi mystics included not only the propagation of the Islamic faith but also the spread of trade throughout the globe. These Sufi orders, as well as individual men who promoted the new faith of Islam, were one of the key contributing factors in the advancement of Islam in Africa. They took on the responsibility of the disciple/teacher relationship and introduced the mystical branch of Islamic science. They incorporated a combination of acknowledgment to the founder of the movement and *dhikr* (remembrance to God). The Tijaniyya, Qadriyya, and, later, the Muridiyya brotherhoods all developed followings in West Africa. Each of these orders had certain doctrines that the student implemented in his everyday life.[34] These orders flourished throughout the Muslim world and played key roles through their ritual and ceremonial practices.[35]

Sufism became a very important methodology and practice within both West Africa and, later, America. This science within Islam became a medium for African appropriation of Islam. Through its exoteric and esoteric practices for both the newly initiated and the seasoned Muslim, Sufism allowed for a combination of Islamic and pre-Islamic practices and offerings while remaining highly orthodox and structured.

As mentioned briefly above, West Africa is home to three major Sufi orders: the Qadriyya, the Tijaniyya, and the Muridiyya. While each of these distinct orders is unique, they all share similar traits, including their focus on the Qur'an, the *hadith*, and the classical Sufi traditions that they use to create their own individualized West African identity. In addition to Sufism, it is important to understand the importance of how Arabic literacy, Sufism, and religious revivalism go hand in hand in West Africa. For members of African societies where oral traditions predominated, Arabic was the first written language to which they were exposed. The term "Ajami," which means "foreign" in Arabic, was the name for the process by which individuals conversant in Arabic through religious education were able to use the Arabic script to communicate in local languages. In West Africa today, Ajami script is used with twenty-nine languages including Wolof, Bambara, Yoruba, Kanuri, and Soninke. According to the historian Hamu al-Arawani Sudani, "converts to Islam might have started to transcribe their language with the Arabic script as early as the twelfth century, when they began to preach their religion among their kin."[36] In *History of Hausa Islamic Verses*, Mervyn Hiskett, a specialist in Hausa language, classifies the themes of Ajami verses in eight categories:[37]

1. Preaching (*waazi*); writing on asceticism (*zuhudi*); writings about death and resurrection, specifically the interrogations that the dead undergo in the grave; reward and punishment; the Day of Judgment.
2. Panegyrica (*madihi*), which are writings praising the Prophet Muhammad and saints.
3. Theology (*tawihi*), which includes didactic explanations on the attributes of God and some basic principles of Muslim theology.
4. Jurisprudence (*fikhi*), which deals with the precepts of Islamic law and concerns personal behavior, particular prayers, ablutions, and successions.
5. Hagiography (*sira*), which concerns the miraculous biography of the Prophet Muhammad and his companions.
6. History (*tarikh*), which includes chronicles concerning the history of the region.
7. Astrology (*ilmin nujumi*) and numerology (*hisabi*), which deal with the evaluation of auspicious days for undertaking projects.
8. Secular texts of political nature and invocations.

The emphasis on Arabic literacy is important as it provides insights into the localization of Arabic as a tool for religious advancement. Just as the Latin script was adapted for local languages in Christian nations with no previous writing system, Islam introduced classical Arabic script to Sub-Saharan Africa and provided a useful tool for religious purposes such as writing prayers and magical protective formulae as well as disseminating religious materials for secular functions such as commercial and administrative recordkeeping;

eulogies; and family matters, including deaths, births, weddings, and such. Fallou Ngom, in his masterfully written work *Muslims beyond the Arab World*, writes, "While there is no comprehensive census of Ajami users in Africa, in some predominately Muslim countries the rates of Ajami literates who do not read, write, or speak either European languages or Arabic are higher than the proportion who are literate in those languages."[38] Ngom further highlights a study by UNESCO that indicates that 38 percent of African adults (some 153 million) are illiterate, of whom two-thirds are women, and that adult literacy is below 50 percent in many Sub-Saharan African countries. But, as Ngom argues, this does not take into consideration local literacies in Ajami.[39] This becomes problematic in regards to how the strongly Western-influenced international community is not privy to the wealth of scholarship afforded to Ajami-trained individuals and requires us to reconsider how we look at West African Islamic knowledge and its contribution in the historical period. Furthermore, the Arabic script and Islamic faith underwent an enrichment process during the localization of Islam in West Africa.

I argue that the Sufi orders in West Africa, particularly those under the influence of Ahmadu Bamba and Ibrahim Niasse, facilitate a local dynamic of institutionalizing the religion of Islam by making it more palatable in their local context. Similarly, Ngom highlights the influence of Ajami in the local context, describing it as the "Ajamization of Islam," which is a better usage of the syncretic term.[40] He argues that the term "Ajamization" is used primarily to address the limitations of syncretism and to expand the work of other specialists on Islam in Africa regarding the Africanization of Islam in Sub-Saharan Africa. Ngom highlights that Ajamization operates throughout the Muslim world, where the Arabic script was enriched in tangible ways in the same manner in which the Islamic faith was enriched.

Finally, Ngom argues that Ajami allowed for the enrichment of Arabic, changing it from a system with only three vowels to a system capable of writing eight vowels for Wolof and five vowels for Hausa. This tangible innovation, in Ngom's view, provided an Ajamization of Arabic, but it is often unacknowledged by Islamic, African, and Western scholars alike as a legitimate contribution. The utility of West African scholars to infuse Ajami as a tool of agency and enrichment provides one of the best examples of the legacy and contribution of West African Islamic intellectual scholarship.

This three-pronged approach of Ajamization, Sufism, and revivalism in West Africa serves as an important tool to demonstrate a centuries-old tradition of pacifism and a nonviolent form of Islamic resistance using local spiritual Islamic leaders. Through the examples of Al Hajj Salim Suwari, Ibrahim Niasse, and Amadou Bamba Mbacke, we are provided insights into how local Islamic leaders sought to tailor Islam to address their local circumstances in Sub-Saharan Africa.

REVIVAL AND RENEWAL

Studies of modern Islamic thought often place Islamic revival movements in the eighteenth century. This reference point often highlights the puritanical ideas of the later Islamic movement known as Wahhabism, a reform movement that has been the intellectual backbone behind fundamentalist interpretations seeking to regain the purity of Islam as practiced during the time of Muhammad. This idea in Islamic history has largely centered specifically on abiding by the Qur'an and Sunna, returning to original teachings of Islam, reviving ijtihad and hadith studies, rejecting innovation and imitation (*taqlid*) in matters of law, and rejecting the excess of Sufi doctrine.[41]

The Arabic terms *ihya* (revival), *tajdid* (renewal), and *islah* (reform) are often used concurrently to address a sense of reawakening of certain Islamic beliefs and practices. These ideas are rooted in the prophetic traditions within Islam that say that a reformer or revivalist would come at the beginning of each century to renew the faith and practices of Muslims. Throughout the world, societies have highlighted the roles of these individuals and their influence within their societies as they sought to bring about new interpretations rooted in the time-honored traditions of their faith.[42]

Many of these reformers are identified by their followers as "renewers" (*mujadid*) who come at appropriate times within countries, societies, and local communities. Abu Hamid al Ghazali (1058–1111), in his famous compendium *Ihya Ulum Al Din* (the revival of Islamic sciences), addresses the ideas of strengthening the spiritual dimensions of faith and practice, and he is often referenced as a Muslim thinker for his expansive areas of knowledge ranging from religious to scientific and secular. Individuals in the nineteenth and twentieth centuries such as Muhammad Abduh and Jamal Al Din Al Afghani focused on educational, religious, and legal reform. Abduh stated, "I went to the West and saw Islam, but no Muslims. I got back to the East and saw Muslims, but no Islam."[43] This further drives home the tension arising between Islamic jurists and reformers who sought to adjust the changing dynamics of the Islamic community and ways to adapt toward the contemporary challenges of its time. Many of the reform/revivalist movements did not call for Westernization but for the acceptance of borrowing modern knowledge from the West within Islamic cultural and religious frameworks. Furthermore, revivalists have debated the concept of ijtihad (individual inquiry in legal matters) and, in many instances, agreed that there is a continuous need for it as shown by the stagnation of the Muslim world and its inability to be flexible or creative in order to adapt to the times.

In many instances in West Africa, revivalism came in the form of mystics preaching for spiritual jihad to address short- and long-term change. However, we would be remiss to say that there were no moments of conquest and violent actions by those who argued that violence was the only means to progress. One such example was the revivalist Islamic cleric and scholar Al Hajj Salim Suwari, an ethnic Soninke who lived during the fifteenth century in present-day Mali. Even today, the majority of West African Sunni scholars trace the lineage (*isnad*) of their knowledge (*ilm*) to Suwari, and it is within this tradition that the distinctive wearing of the turban became popular within the West African Muslim religious authority. Suwari is known to have institutionalized the study and teachings of two core Maliki religious texts: the *Muwatta* of Imam Malik and the *Shifa* of the twelfth-century scholar Ayyad ibn Musa, a Mali judge from the Iberian Peninsula. Suwari's role as an Islamic reformer was in his support for the rights of non-Muslims in Muslim-majority populations.

This progressive view was rather revolutionary at the time. Suwari argued that God alone decides who He wants to guide to belief (*iman*) or disbelief (*kufr*), and Muslims should set an example by living peacefully among non-Muslims and nonbelievers and should not actively proselytize (*dawa*). Jeffrey Halverson, in an article detailing Suwari in the *Journal of Muslim Minority Affairs,* states, "Muslims are permitted to fully accept non-Muslim political authority (as social order is preferable to disorder), so long as their ability to practice Islam on an individual level is not obstructed."[44] This understanding will become critical as we explore in detail the experience of enslaved African Muslims like Salih Bilali, who resided in the state of Georgia and who was an enslaved African living in a non-Muslim society.

Provided below are examples of two West African thinkers and personalities, Shaykh Amadou Bamba Mbacke and Shaykh Ibrahim Niasse, as the archetypes of Islamic revivalist thought using local adaptation. Perhaps the most influential Muslim leaders of Sub-Saharan Africa, these leaders used the process of Ajamization, Sufism, and Islamic revivalism to further deepen existing and new adherents to the faith in order to expand a living tradition of spirituality that could address the needs and concerns of West African society.

AHMADU BAMBA MBAKE

Ahmadu Bamba Mbake (1853–1927) established his foothold in 1883 in present-day Senegal. He was the founder and leader of the Muridiyya Sufi order. This order is unique in that its origins, identity, and later patron saint is African; unlike most other orders, it does not trace its origins or roots back to Arab or North African Sufi scholars. In West Africa, the Qadiriyya and Tijaniyya were the largest Sufi orders, and each had its own unique, specialized Arabic prayers and spiritual formulas. Having been born in Senegal, Bamba memorized the Qur'an as a young child, as was typical within West African Muslim communities. He was a rebel, however, in the sense that he originally received and was initiated into the Tijaniyya Sufi order and went on to create the Muridiyya order, but only after being initiated into the Qadiriyya order as well. What Bamba articulates in the creation of the Muridiyya order is a need for an emerging legitimacy, independence, and agency in the context of French colonial rule in Senegal. The French colonial administrations labeled Bamba an anticolonialist and both subjected him to house imprisonment and exiled him from Senegal numerous times. He was exiled to Gabon from 1895 to 1902 and then to Mauritania from 1903 to 1907, after which the French deprived Bamba of freedom of movement for three decades. This experience, as later evident in the spiritual techniques and practices of adherents of the Muridiyya order, served to demonstrate elements of community and societal resilience in the face of adversity.

For Bamba, the Qur'an served as a basis for all of his doctrinal practices. Although he was labeled as an anticolonialist, followers of Bamba would argue that colonization was incidental and treat his practices and rituals as part of a long odyssey toward sainthood.[45] This idea of sainthood is a common theme within Muridiyya literature and offers a practical understanding of Bamba. For the Muridiyya, sainthood is not a matter of institutional jurisdiction; instead, it is based on personal spiritual attainment, and it cannot be transferred. It is a system based on the cultivation of a following.[46] Through a series of time-honored Sufi spiritual techniques and practices, Bamba and the Muridiyya established a cultural and religious revivalism that now has transnational boundaries.

One famous Sufi poet gives expression to Bamba's role as an Islamic spiritual guide rooted in an environment with a predominance of Qadiri and Tijani shaykhs, his slow resistance, and his desire to create an independent religious community addressing the needs and struggles of the Senegalese and the larger West African Muslim populations:

> I no longer need either Baghdad or Fez,
> On Seeing Jolof, I submitted entirely.[47]

Bamba was not without his detractors, however, particularly because he had also received the Tijani *wird*.[48] A wird is a litany or repetition used for daily practices of remembrance for the Sufi initiate. These daily practices are vital for membership into Sufi orders, and each *tariqa* has a unique set of litanies, either consisting of Qur'anic Arabic texts or a combination of Qur'anic texts and divinely inspired Arabic poetry authored by shaykhs of Sufi orders.

Bamba gradually abandoned the Tijani wird, which was, in his words, the last foreign wird he would use. This was taken by some to imply that he had reached the same rank as Ahmad Tijani, the founder of the Tijani order, which was blasphemy for adherents, but it also demonstrated a slow independence emerging from Bamba's teachings. Bamba was later initiated into the

Qadiri tariqa. Nevertheless, according to Cheikh Anta Babou in his historical analysis of Amadu Bamba and the founding of the Muridiyya, despite having mastered the classical texts and traveled to Mauritania and other places of Islamic learning,

> Amadu Bamba most likely experienced how fraternity between Muslims, especially Muslim clerics—so celebrated in the Quran and the prophetic traditions—could be ambiguous in practices when it involved people of different skin colors and cultures. Sidyya Baba and his Moorish compatriots did not have much regard for their black colleagues on the other side of the Senegal River.[49]

To further amplify this point, Paul Marty, a French colonial administrator and writer on Islam in West Africa, highlights that Sidiyya Baba writes in a letter: "The Blacks think of themselves as Muslims, however the majority among them do not have the slightest correct notion of what Islam is really about, they ignore the Islamic ethic, its law and principles. But we (the Moors in our capacity as teachers and guides) have a responsibility to bear in this situation."[50]

In the preamble to his book *Massalik Al-Jinan,* Bamba wrote, "Do not let my condition of a black man mislead you about the virtue of this work," because, he continued, "the best of man before God, without discrimination, is the one who fears Him the most" and "skin color cannot be the cause of stupidity or ignorance."[51] As Babou notes, the engagement and treatment of Bamba in the lands of the Arabs had proved that his future was better off in his homeland of Senegal.[52]

Bamba's philosophical, spiritual, and practical teachings were rooted in a revivalism of nationalism and self-determination that stemmed from being an African Muslim. It is through this experience and independence that Bamba articulates critical thinking and independence in West Africa.

IBRAHIM NIASSE

Ibrahim Niasse (1900–1975) was a West African Islamic scholar from modern-day Senegal and a sage of the Tijaniyya Sufi order. As a disciple of the Moroccan-born Ahmed Tijani, the founder of the Tijaniyya order, Niasse was versed in the spiritual practices of the order including its special emphasis on Islamic law, jurisprudence, and Sufism. Like other West African Muslim students, Niasse studied the West African Islamic curriculum at the time including the *Risala, Murshid al Mu'in,* and *Muwatta* as well as various works on Sufism including Ibn Ata Allah's *Hikam* and Ali Harazim's *Jawahir al Ma'ani,* the most authoritative work on the life and teachings of Ahmed Tijani. In addition, Niasse was instructed in Qur'anic interpretation, which is usually taught at the very end of a long training. One may argue that Niasse is considered one of the most prolific and notable West African Islamic scholars along with Bamba. Niasse's writings build on a regional tradition of demonstrating sophisticated and complex esoteric and Islamic knowledge by an Islamic revivalist and challenging the colonial-era prejudice and repeated disdain for black African Islamic scholars.[53] The perceived inferiority of West African Islamic scholars is an oft-repeated narrative that scholars of the continent of Africa were up against. West African Islamic revivalists like Niasse challenge this pervasive attitude through their prolific writings by offering critiques of external non-Muslim opponents and internal Muslim critics who seek to discredit and challenge African Islamic scholarship and the emergent West African Islamic thought. Niasse used the practice of *tarbiya* (spiritual training) as the path to guide his adherents to experience knowledge and to develop a work ethic that made his influence practical. Niasse's emphasis on teaching adaptive and pluralistic Islamic legal rulings and providing a practical religious message for the common man allowed him to have a larger influence in the subregion, including Mauritania, Nigeria, Ghana, and Senegal, and even in the larger African diaspora as well as with Western-born converts. Furthermore, his universal message addressed more directly those people who, like his own family, were born into a lower class status, and it showed his egalitarian spirit and the inspiration he provided to all members of West African Islamic society.[54] His nonaristocratic background is often cited as having been a factor in what made the movement attractive.[55]

Furthermore, Niasse's influence took place under the backdrop of the colonial period. His influence, along with his practical interpretation of Sufi doctrine, allowed him to build on the traditions of the teachings of the founder of the Tijaniyya order (though not without the founder's criticism) and directly address the realities of his native Senegambia and the larger West African society. Africanist academic Dr. John Paden refers to Niasse's influence as "reformed Tijaniyya," describing his influence as a regurgitation of the work of Ahmed Tijani.

However, Rudiger Seesemann challenges this notion in his work *The Divine Flood,* calling it misleading as it suggests that Niasse departed from the Tijani tradition. Seesemann argues instead that Niasse built on the teachings of the Tijaniyya while addressing the needs and concerns of his community. This argument seems particularly appropriate as Niasse actually emerged out of a generation of three great Muslim saints of the wider region of Senegambia whose religious institutions, ideas, and influence can be seen in the contemporary era. These saints, Abdallah Niasse, Malik Uthman Sy, and Ahamdu Bamba, offered spiritual and economic stability to rural populations and ultimately revolutionized the consciousness of West African Islamic society. Ibrahim Niasse and these saints offered a departure from the traditional religious leaders and African rulers, as well as the leaders of jihad movements and the colonial class, as they sought to transcend rigid and pervasive social boundaries and hierarchies. Additionally, Niasse built on the theme throughout Islamic classical sources of anticipating the emergence of a great religious leader, or *Mujadid*, a reviver or renewer of Islam who only comes once every hundred years to aid the Muslim community. As will be seen in later chapters, this tradition of Islamic revivalism is the cornerstone to Islamic thought, and it is rooted in a classical tradition of renewal and revaluation for each generation in communities throughout the world who adhere to this idea.

NOTES

1. Zakaria Bashier, *Sunshine at Madinah*. (United Kingdom: Islamic Foundation, 1990).
2. Michael Gomez, *Reversing Sail: History of the African Diaspora* (New York: Cambridge University Press, 2005).
3. Arabic Qur'an 30:22.
4. Arabic Qur'an, 49:13.
5. This is the famous last farewell sermon of the Prophet Muhammad. This is also illustrated with Muhammad Haykal, *The Life of Muhammad* (Kuala Lumpur: Islamic Book Trust, 1994.)
6. Arnold J. Toynbee, *A Study of History*, vol. 1 (London: Oxford University Press, 1939), 266.
7. Al Lat and Al Uzza are considered to be two prominent smaller gods in the hierarchy of religious practices of pagan Arab society.
8. Curtis, *The Call of Bilal*.
9. al-Jahiz, *Fakhr as-Sudan*, in A. S. M. Harun, ed., *Rasa'il al-Jahiz* (Cairo, 1964), 1: 216, lists all the many black peoples.
10. *Diwan*, ed. Maymani (Cairo, 1369/1950), p. 26.
11. Ibid.
12. Translated by E. van Donzel in his article "Ibn al-Jawzi on Ethiopians in Baghadad," in *The Islamic World from Classical to Modern Times*, ed. A. L. Udovitch (Princeton, NJ: Darwin Press, 1989), 113.
13. Rudolph T. Ware III, *The Walking Quran: Islamic Education, Embodied Knowledge, and History in West Africa* (Chapel Hill: University of North Carolina Press, 2014), 5.
14. Bernard Lewis, *Race and Slavery in the Middle East: An Historical Enquiry* (New York: Oxford University Press, 1990).
15. Peter Clarke, *West Africa and Islam* (London: Edward Arnold, 1982).
16. Clarke, *West Africa and Islam*, 12–65.
17. Ware, *The Walking Quran*, 147.
18. Ware, *The Walking Qu'ran*.
19. Nehemiah Levtzion, *Ancient Ghana and Mali* (New York: Africana Publishing Company, 1980).
20. Ibn Battuta, "Audiences of the Sultan of Mali," in *Documents from the African Past*, ed. Robert O. Collins (Princeton: Markus Wiener, 2009), 15.
21. Kane, *Beyond Timbuktu*.
22. Brent D. Singleton, "African Bibliophiles: Books and Libraries in Medieval Timbuktu," *Libraries and Culture* 39, no. 1 (2004).
23. Lamin Sanneh, *Beyond Jihad: The Pacifist Tradition in West African Islam* (New York: Oxford University Press, 2016).

24. *Al Muqaddimah al Izziyah* is a treatise on Maliki Fiqh. Abu Hasan al Shadili is the author, and its text is considered a classical body of work among adherents of the Maliki school of thought.

25. D. F. Eickelman, *Knowledge and Power in Morocco: The Education of a Twentieth-Century Notable* (Princeton, NJ: Princeton University Press, 1992), 56.

26. Diane Simpson, "Syncretism in Two African Cultures," *University of Western Ontario Journal of Anthropology* 2, no. 1 (2011): 61.

27. Asim Roy, *The Islamic Syncretist Tradition in Bengal* (Princeton, NJ: Princeton University Press, 1983), 8.

28. David Robinson, *Muslim Societies in African History: New Approaches to African History* (Cambridge: Cambridge University Press, 2004).

29. See Louis Brenner, "The Histories of Religion in Africa," *Journal of Religion in Africa* 30, no. 2 (January 2000).

30. The terms "tasawwuf" and "Sufism" are often used interchangeably in English texts in reference to Islamic spirituality.

31. Ahmad Iyad, *Al Tasawwuf al Islami* (Cairo, 1970), 62.

32. See Carl Ernst and Bruce Lawrence, *Sufi Martyrs of Love* (New York: Palgrave Macmillan, 2002).

33. See Rudiger Seesemann, *The Divine Flood: Ibrahim Niasse and the Roots of a Twentieth-Century Sufi Revival* (New York: Oxford University Press, 2011).

34. Jamil Abun-Nasr, *The Tijaniyya: A Sufi Order in the Modern World* (New York: Oxford University Press, 1965).

35. J. Spencer Trimingham, *The Sufi Orders in Islam* (Oxford: Clarendon Press, 1971).

36. See Ousmane Kane's *Beyond Timbuktu* and Mahmud Hamu, *Al-Kashf an al-makhtutat al-arabiyya wa al-maktubat bil-harf al arabi fi mintaqat al sahil al-Ifriqi*, manuscript, n.d. (Timbuktu).

37. Hamid Bobboyi, "Ajami Literature and the Study of the Sokoto Caliphate," in *The Meanings of Timbuktu* ed., Shamil Jeppie and Souleymane Bachir Diagne (Cape Town: HSRC Press, 2008), 123–33; Mervyn Hiskett, *A History of Hausa Islamic Verse* (London: University of London School of Oriental and African Studies, 1975).

38. Ngom, *Muslims Beyond the Arab World*.

39. "Literacy and Non-formal Eudcation," UNESCO Office, Dakar, accessed December 29, 2016, http://unesdoc.unesco.org/images/0014/001446/144656e.pdf.

40. Ngom, *Muslims Beyond the Arab World*.

41. There is a plethora of writing on this topic. Fazlur Rahman, *Islam* (Chicago: University of Chicago Press, 1968), 242–50; and John Esposito, "Tradition and Modernization in Islam," in *Movements and Issues in World Religions*, ed. Charles Wei-hsun Fu and Gerhard Spiegler (New York: Greenwood Press, 1987).

42. Ahmad Dallal, "The Origins and Objectives of Islamic Revivalist Thought, 1750–1850," *Journal of American Oriental Society* 113, no. 3 (1993), 341–59.

43. Oliver Learman, *An Introduction to Classical Islamic Philosophy* (New York: Cambridge University Press, 1985).

44. See Jeffrey R. Halverson, "West African Islam in Colonial and Antebellum South Carolina," *Journal of Muslim Minority Affairs* 36, no. 3 (August 2016).

45. This idea of sainthood should not be seen in a Christian (Catholic) perspective. Sainthood or holiness shouldn't be seen in solely outerworldly means; according to Bamba, sainthood is a personal spiritual attainment and cannot be transferred.

46. Trimingham, *The Sufi Orders of Islam*, 48, 225.

47. Khadim Mbacke, *Sufism and Religious Brotherhoods in Senegal* (Princeton, NJ: Markus Wiener Publishers, 2005), 49.

48. Devotion or liturgy specific to a Sufi order. Specialized prayers in which the Sufi order is defined through Qur'anic passages or Arabic prayers as created by the founder of this order. The initiate of the order is given the secret *wird* of the order upon completion of the training, transferring the spiritual power of the chain of transmission from the founder of the order and Muhammad to the initiate.

49. Cheikh Anta Babou, *Fighting the Greater Jihad: Amadu Bamba and the Founding of the Muridiyya of Senegal, 1852–1913* (Athens: Ohio University Press, 2007), 62.
50. Ibid.
51. Amadu Bamba Mbacke, *Massalik Al-Jinaan* (Rabat: Dar El Kitab, 1984), 28.
52. Ibid., 62–63.
53. Zachary Wright, "The Kashif al Ilbas of Shaykh Ibrahim Niasse: An Analysis of the Text," *Journal of Islamic Africa* 1, no. 1 (2010), 110. http://www.academia.edu/6000096/The_K%C4%81shif_al-Ilb%C4%81s_of_Shaykh_Ibr%C4%81him_Niasse_Analysis_of_the_Text.
54. Rudiger Seesemann, *The Divine Flood: Ibrahim Niasse and the Roots of a Twentieth-Century Sufi Revival* (New York: Oxford University Press, 2011), 153.
55. Rüdiger Seesemann, *The Divine Flood: Ibrahim Niasse and the Roots of a Twentieth-Century Sufi Revival*, (Oxford University Press: Oxford), 2011.

Chapter Three

Africanizing Dixie

The Enslaved African Muslim Experience and the Black American Islamic Continuum

THE ENSLAVED AFRICAN EXPERIENCE

Between the early 1500s and 1866, more than 12.5 million Africans were transported in bondage to the Americas, and, of those, around 10.7 million survived the middle passage. The vast majority of those enslaved Africans arrived not in North America but in the Caribbean and South America, especially Brazil. Regardless of the exact number of individuals forced into bondage, the importation of African human merchandise to the Americas made a sizable imprint on the economics of soon-to-be American society.[1] Many of these colonies, some which eventually had direct shipment to the Southern shores of North America, impacted many lives and traditions. These colonies not only became profitable states for the Southern economy but also increased the size of the population in the American South.

The historical academic literature points to a consistent theme of Southern planters seeking to separate men, women, and children along ethnic lines. They encouraged mixing the African population in order to discourage a homogenous cluster of people, which could potentially create divisions among the enslaved African population. Families with the last names of Mende, Bantu, and Yoruba, to name a few, were all clustered together into one monolithic flow, resulting in the creation of one identity.[2] In Brazil, the *Male* ("Muslim") uprising in 1835 was a product of tribal and ethnic lines uniting and establishing a revolt against colonial Portuguese society.[3] Mechal Sobel notes in his work that it was "trader lore that slave populations should be mixed so that they might not have a *lingua franca* and would be forced to learn English more rapidly."[4] In many instances, enslaved Africans were consistently being imported from specific regions in West Africa for their technical expertise. Enslaved Africans from the West African coast were essential to plantation owners as they were familiar with the climate and vegetation of the southern American states. Men and women from present-day Senegal and Gambia were particularly useful because of their skilled techniques in indigo and rice cultivation.[5] Both of these crops grew in the low country of South Carolina, and precise accuracy was required for growing them. Peter Wood, a noted historian of blacks in South Carolina, argues that, during the eighteenth century, roughly 40 percent of the Africans coming into the thirteen colonies passed through Charleston.[6] Equally important, this large percentage provided this coastal city with a continuous stream of cargo until 1808, when federal law prohibited the transportation of slaves through the Atlantic slave trade.[7] The American South, particularly South Carolina, was perhaps the epicenter of activity for the importation of African-born slaves, and it later became the location where large concentrations of African Muslims' public and written records have been found.

The shipment of African-born slaves peaked in the mid-to-late eighteenth century and again briefly at the start of the nineteenth century. Between 1761 and 1775, nearly 57,000 enslaved Africans were imported to South Carolina, with the greatest number arriving in the five-year period between 1771 and 1775 (19,215 total). According to slave shipping databases at Emory University, vessels carrying the slaves embarked from various locations in West Africa, including Congo, Angola, Senegambia, Sierra Leone, and Ghana, to name a few.[8]

AFRICANIZING THE SOUTH

We describe a two-phase process for the evolution of the enslaved African population's struggle and their resistance against Southern plantation owners' attempts at forced assimilation and conversion to Christianity. The first phase was the rejection and attempted hidden conversion to Christianity via the spiritual Islamic sciences taught in West Africa, and the second phase was through the Gullah/Geechee tradition developed in the American South as a form of resistance against white southern plantation owners. We will see in this chapter how this resistance was engaged directly via key personalities and the Gullah/Geechee communities of low-country South Carolina and Georgia.

As in West Africa, the African religious beliefs and practices brought to the Americas were varied and numerous. A significant portion of West African– and continental African–based populations were Muslim, and many of the enslaved Africans who journeyed to the New World served as living testimonies to these traditions. The earliest research of African Muslims in America can be found in the sales records of European slave companies. Many ships carrying enslaved Africans came up and down the Eastern Seaboard of the United States with the highest concentration arriving in the American South. Islam had established a stronghold in West Africa and was now seeking to plant a seed in the Americas. Various records from newspapers and census reports have indicated that men and women who were of Islamic background were in clear sight and present in the American plantation system. Leo Weiner, who was a professor of ethno-linguistics at Harvard University in the early twentieth century, asserts that there were interactions between West Africans and indigenous Native Americans living in the Gulf of Mexico region.[9] Even though he did not have much evidence other than some words and personal testimonies of the indigenous population, his point would be given some validity less than a century later.

For enslaved communities in the American South, holding on to their religious identity in the colonial period was not easy. Plantation owners were careful to introduce Christian religious instruction as a process of acculturation for enslaved Africans. Conversion to Christianity was perhaps the most widespread method by which African Muslims were quickly assimilated and forced to form new communal relations. Scholars have limited information to piece together concerning when the open practice of Islam ceased in the American South, but it is clear that the American-born children of African Muslims seem to have not widely practiced Islam, nor did they identify as Muslims.[10] Furthermore, ideas of antiblackness and Arab superiority, evident throughout early global Islamic history and on the continent of Africa, were also techniques applied in America. Kambiz GhaneaBassiri, in his book *A History of Islam in America,* argues how "de-negrofication" and "de-Islamization" were strategies employed in the New World so as to strip enslaved Africans of their identity and to encourage self-hate techniques that allowed them to distance themselves from their African features and attributes. GhaneaBassiri uses the examples of historical African Muslim personalities in America to drive home his point. The following are just a few examples: Thomas Bluett, the biographer of Job Ben Solomon, an enslaved African Muslim, wrote of Job, "his Countenance was exceedingly pleasant, yet grave and composed; his hair was long, black and curled, being very different from that of the Negroes commonly brought from Africa."[11] Omar Ibn Said, who will be explored later, is described as an "Arabian prince . . . a hereditary prince of the Foulah tribe in Arabia."[12] In addition, the depiction of Ibrahima Abdul Rahman, a prince from West Africa, is recorded by Cyrus Griffin, the editor of the *Natchez Southern Galaxy* in Mississippi:

> That Prince [Abdul Rahman's slave name] is a Moor, there can be but little doubt. He is six feet in height; and though sixty-five years of age he has the

vigor of the meridian of life. When he arrived in this country, his hair hung in flowing ringlets far below his shoulder. Much against his will, his master compelled him to submit to sheers, and this ornament which the Moor would part with in his own country only with his life, since that time he has entirely neglected. It has become coarse, and in some degree curly. His skin, also, by long service in the sun, and the privations of bondage, has been materially changed; and his whole appearance indicates the Foolah rather than the Moor. But Prince states explicitly, and with an air of pride that not a drop of negro blood runs in his veins. He places the Negro in a scaled being infinitely below the Moor.[13]

I argue that the notions of Moor and Arab were, for the majority of Americans, based on popular literature of the time, including Shakespeare's *Othello*. The depiction in Othello and much of American literature was based on Europeans' perspectives, and they oftentimes lacked careful nuances based on race and geographic location. As GhaneaBassiri highlights, "African Muslims were painfully aware of the oppressive linkage slavery reinforced between one's color and humanity."[14] These carefully constructed dehumanization tactics employed by white plantation owners and their proxy stewards would serve as effective deterrent mechanisms to enslaved Africans and, later, would bolster the attempt to convert them to Christianity.

In his book *Slave Religion*, Albert Raboteau describes a concerted effort to establish plantation religious missions in the American South, both to save the souls of slaves and their masters and to Christianize them. While it seems clear that the practice of Islam died out among second-generation African Americans, the conversion of Muslims to Christianity had already begun with the first generation of arrivals. Abdul Rahman and another enslaved African by the name of Lamine Kaba responded to the American Colonization Society, a popular evangelical movement at the time that sought to establish a Christian colony in Africa. They both were baptized, and they promised to spread Christian values upon their return to their native homeland. Mahommah Gardo Baquaqua, originally from Benin and enslaved in America, was also reported to have converted to Christianity "to be enabled to return to his native land, to instruct his own people in the ways of the Gospel of Christ."[15] The historical records of Muslims who traveled back to Africa further corroborates the notion that they perhaps pretended to convert to Christianity in order to comply with the environment in which they found themselves and to return back home.[16]

Over time, African retentions combined with adaptations to American slavery led to the formation of uniquely African American cultures and identities, including the Gullah Geechee tradition. During and after slavery, Gullah and Geechee individuals passed on cultural traditions from one generation to the next through language, agriculture, and spirituality, including the early influences of their African Muslim ancestors. Among the low country's

Gullah and Geechee enslaved African populations, there was an incredibly diverse religious community that included a fusion of traditional African religious traditions and Islamic traditions. For these enslaved African populations, retention of West African religious and cultural traditions was a key part of their cultural tradition preserved since the mid-1700s. The communities and individuals who reside today along the coast of the southeastern United States continue to share similar cultural and linguistic connections to West Africa and are often referred to as Gullah/Geechee.

For those living in the low country of South Carolina and Georgia, "Gullah" often described the culture of the emergent African American community life, including food, customs, and traditions passed on from their ancestors who made the middle passage journey to the Americas. The term "Geechee" captures the language spoken, a mix between a patois and Pidgin English with an infusion of West African dialect and language primarily from the Mano River countries of Sierra Leone, Guinea, and Liberia. Many traditions of the Gullah and Geechee culture were passed from one generation to the next through language, agriculture, and spirituality.

Unfortunately, as of this writing, the vast majority of scholarly research in the area of the intersection between enslaved Africans in America, the Gullah/Geechee tradition, and West African Islam has been scarce at best. In Margaret Washington's Creel book, *A Peculiar People: Slave Religion and Community Culture among the Gullah*, the author makes little to no mention of the connection between enslaved Africans in America and Islam in general or the mystical experiences of West African Sufism in particular. Furthermore, Ras Michael Brown's *African-Atlantic Cultures and the South Carolina Lowcountry* makes no mention of Islam leaving West Africa or entering the larger Americas. This lack of details by scholars regarding an Islamic presence within the Gullah/Geechee tradition in South Carolina and Georgia demonstrates a limited understanding of West African spirituality or the impact of Islam on the continent of Africa. The examples provided here reflect varying degrees of local custom, oral traditions, and syncretic incorporation of pre-Islamic religion and behaviors. This is of particular importance as West African Sufism played an important role in the development of Islamic communities on the continent of Africa.

The pre-Islamic African traditions oftentimes coexisted with Islam and provided interwoven and sometimes fluid religious interpretation as demonstrated by the living and experiential form of Sufism, which historically favored a heavy emphasis on esoteric readings of the Qur'an and Sunna. By considering the impact of West African Muslims on the African continent and their New World descendants of the low country, I build on the research of Dr. Jeffrey Halverson that highlights the relationship between Gullah Praise Houses in the low country and West African Sufi circles, or *zawiyaas,* which would have initially existed alongside traditional houses of worship in

America. Zawiyaas are locations designed for Muslims who seek to go into sincere and passionate overtime in their religious practices and engage in Islamic devotional chanting and, sometimes, Islamically sanctioned rhythmic movement for the remembrance of Allah and the acquisition of experiential knowledge.[17] In many Sufi orders, a state of divine presence is summoned, and the individual's soul is believed to be absorbed into the essence of the oneness of Allah. The Qadiri tariqa, well-known in West Africa, utilizes chanting and distinctly circular gatherings engaged in rhythmic movements, including swaying, bowing, and clapping, in their rituals. In many instances, new initiates in the tariqa are given wirds, personal formulas akin to mantras, from their teacher or guide to use in their daily lives. In the cases of the enslaved African Muslims Yarrow Mamout, Omar Ibn Said, Ibrahima Abdur Rahman, and Salih Bilali, the formal and informal Gullah Praise Houses utilized their personal wirds brought from West Africa to help them survive in the American South. These wirds also served as mnemonic devices that the adherent could use for the purpose of elaborative encoding, retrieval cues, and imagery that allowed the brain to have better retention of the information. These encoded meanings within the wird itself provide multiple meanings and knowledge for those versed in its power and access. While one level of understanding might be widely shared inside and outside a community, additional layers of interpretation may be known only to a select group, therefore conveying a certain nuanced meaning.

Another potential link between the Gullah tradition and Sufism involves the commonly called Ring-Shout ritual that occurs in the Praise Houses. During this ritual, adherents sing aloud in an act of devotional praise, as many Sufis do in their devotional practices. I would suggest, however, that these connections between these religious traditions go even deeper. Many scholars, including Lorenzo Dow Turner, have concluded that the English word "shout" is derived from the Arabic *saut*, which means to "raise one's voice." Turner repeatedly argues that the definition of "saut" has its origins in the frequent movement of Muslim worshippers around the *Kaaba* in Mecca, Saudi Arabia. Although this exact definition may be debatable and has been a source of further scholarly inquiry, Turner does move in the right direction on the word's origins, as the circumambulation of the Kaaba is called the *tawaf* and does have an Islamic nexus.[18] In recent decades, modern-day scholars, including Sylvianne Diouf and Jeffrey Halverson, have asserted that the Gullah adoption of *saut* is rooted in Sufi usage to connote sacred sound. Diouf argues that though Turner's definition is rooted in some inaccuracy, there are similarities between West African Sufism and the syncretic shouters found among enslaved Africans in Trinidad and Tobago in the eighteenth and nineteenth centuries. Halverson highlights that the Sufi term *shawq,* as defined by the eleventh-century Sufi teacher Abdul Qasim al-Qushayri, refers to the passionate longing of the heart to meet God. Halverson highlights that these Sufi rituals were emotional and directed toward seeking out encounters with the divine, similar to those practiced at the Gullah Praise Houses in South Carolina and Georgia.[19]

As presented earlier, we have an abundant amount of evidence demonstrating that there were enslaved African Muslims in the low country of South Carolina and Georgia. Some of the best documented accounts by such Muslims have been found in South Carolina, which was arguably the epicenter of enslaved African Muslim activity because of entry ports such as Charleston. South Carolina has also been the source of numerous articles written on Muslim runaway slaves, which have also been recorded in public documents.[20] The *Columbian Herald*, a newspaper from the late eighteenth century, included one such public notice. It read, "1790 (Thursday) the Suffering of Yamboo, and African in South Carolina."[21] Additionally, in the *Charleston Times*, November 17, 1803 (Thursday): "Five dollars Reward. Runaway, a Negro, about 30 years of age. He had on, when he went away, a brown frock coat. He has been accustomed to working as a Gardner at Vauxhall. Whoever will deliver him at the Work House, shall receive the above reward, and all expenses."[22]

The Charleston Vauxhall, an entertainment venue frequented by socialites, was run by a Frenchman named Alexander Placides from 1799 to 1812. The runaway slave, named Mahomet, may have belonged to Placides, or may have come with the property when Placides bought it in around 1798. This raises serious questions about the role of the slave, property ownership, and status.

A Christian enslaved African by the name of Charles Ball, the grandson of an African-born slave in Maryland, recounted that he had met many African Muslims who had disembarked in Charleston. "I knew several [Africans]," he writes, "who must have been, from what I have since learned, Mohamedans; though at that time, I had never heard of the religion of Mohammed."[23] As Halverson argues, "the fact that Ball was unable to identify these slaves as adherents of Islam until late in life is notable for scholars interested in slave narrative, missionary accounts and how observers perceived the religious practices of African slaves."[24] Ball also notes, "there was one man on this plantation, who prayed five times every day, always turning his face to the east, when in the performance of his devotion . . . we were joined by the African born man who prayed five times a day; and at the going down of the sun he stopped and prayed aloud in our hearing, in a language I did not understand."[25] Finally, Major David Anderson, an officer in the American Revolution who owned a plantation along the Tiger River, had enslaved Africans in his possession during the year 1768, one of whom was a literate Muslim who wrote down five short chapters (*surahs*) of the Qur'an in Arabic, including Surah al Fatihah, which is the primary Muslim prayer.[26]

Omar Ibn Said

Omar Ibn Said (1765–1864) was born in present-day Senegal, West Africa. According to his autobiography, Said was captured at the age of thirty-seven and forced to travel to Charleston through the trans-Atlantic slave trade where he was sold into slavery in 1807.

In 1807, the same year he arrived, he escaped, but he was recaptured shortly thereafter and transported to Fayetteville, North Carolina, where he was imprisoned after entering a Christian church to pray. Said received notoriety for writing on the walls of his jail cell in Arabic, an act that challenged the prevailing understanding that enslaved Africans were not able to read and write. Soon after his recapture he became the legal property of General James Owen from North Carolina, who served as the US congressman to the Fifteenth Congress (1817–1819).

While enslaved in America, Said wrote more than a dozen manuscripts, including the only known autobiography written in Arabic by an enslaved African in the United States.

Though never receiving his freedom, his influence was documented throughout academic and other circles of influence of the era. Theodore Dwight, the first secretary of the American Ethnological Society, an early anthropological scholarly institution, was aware of Said and other enslaved African Muslims who were a part of early American society. In 1864, in the middle of the civil war, Dwight noted, "It affords an idea of the degree of education among the Moslem blacks, when we see a man like this able to read and write a language so different from his own native tongue. Where is the youth, or even the adult, among the mass of our people who is able to do the same in Latin or Greek."[27]

Ayyuba Suleiman Diallo

Ayyuba Suleiman Diallo (1701–1773), also known as Job Ben Solomon, was born in Bundu, of present-day Senegal. Job was a *Hafiz*, which meant he memorized the entire Qur'an and came from a prominent Muslim family known for their religious scholarship and understanding of Islamic spiritual sciences.

Job was captured in his homeland in 1730 and brought to Annapolis, Maryland, another major North American port in the trans-Atlantic slave trade, where he was sold into slavery.

Conversant in the Arabic language, Job wrote a letter that he hoped would make its way back to his father via James Oglethorpe, a British aristocrat and founder of the Georgia colony.

Oglethorpe helped purchase Job's freedom and sent him to London, where he worked for the Royal African Company. In 1734, Thomas Bluett, a British lawyer, wrote a detailed account of Job's life:

> His Memory was extraordinary; for when he was fifteen Years old he could say the whole Alcoran [Qur'an] by heart, and while he was here in England he wrote three Copies of it without the Assistance of any other Copy, and without so much as looking to one of those three when he wrote the others. He would often laugh at me when he heard me say I had forgot any Thing, and told me he hardly ever forgot any Thing in his Life, and wondered that any other body should. . . .
> Upon our Talking and making Signs to him, he wrote a Line or two before us, and when he read it, pronounced the words Allah and Mahommed; by which, and his refusing a Glass of Wine we offered him, we perceived he was a Mahometan, but could not imagine of what Country he was, or how he got thither; for by his affable Carriage, and the easy Composure of his Countenance, we could perceive he was no common Slave.[28]

Ibrahima Abdur Rahman

Ibrahima Abdur Rahman (1762–1829) was born in present-day Guinea, West Africa. Ibrahima was a prince in his native homeland, and he was enslaved for forty-two years in Natchez, Mississippi, until his freedom in 1828. Ibrahima was educated in the Islamic intellectual center of Timbuktu and was conversant in the Arabic language. Because of his abilities in Arabic and through a chance meeting with a former British captive, a letter was sent in Arabic via diplomatic channels to the embassy of Morocco, which then sent the communiqué to President John Quincy Adams, who helped facilitate his freedom. With the support of abolitionists and the African Colonization Society, he managed to make his way to Liberia but died before he could make his way back to his homeland of Guinea. Much of the publicly available information on Ibrahima comes from a pamphlet titled, "A Statement with Regards to the Moorish Prince, Abduhl Rahhaman," written by Thomas H. Gallaudet, one of the cofounders of the American School for the Deaf. Ibrahima is known affectionately as the "Prince amongst Slaves" due to his royal African lineage and scholarly credentials.[29]

Yarrow Mamout

Yarrow Mamout (1701–1773) was an enslaved African Muslim, entrepreneur, and property owner in the Georgetown area of Washington, DC. Mamout was captured in his homeland in West Africa at the age of sixteen and arrived in Annapolis, Maryland, on the slave ship *Elijah* in 1752. In 1822 and 1819, respectively, American painters James Simpson and Charles William Peale painted portraits of Mamout, which became the earliest known portraits of an American Muslim. Why Peale painted the picture of Yarrow is unknown, but some assumptions among historians include that Yarrow's peculiarity of being a practicing Muslim circulated through Washington, DC, and Eastern Seaboard elite circles. Peale is also known for his paintings of George Washington. "He professes to be a Mohometan (Muslim) and is often seen and heard in the streets singing praises to God and, conversing with him, he said man is no good unless his religion comes from the heart."[30]

Salih Bilali

Salih Bilali was an enslaved African Muslim from Mali who lived on Sapelo Island in Georgia. He was given the title of plantation manager among other enslaved Africans and is documented as having observed Islamic ritual prayers and fasted during the month of Ramadan. In addition, Bilali was an influential leader who, along with other African Muslims, shaped what would become the Gullah/Geechee traditions on the sea islands of South Carolina and Georgia. Bilali was owned by James Hamilton Couper and lived on his plantation on St. Simons Island in Georgia. Couper allowed his enslaved population to worship freely. As Couper noted about Bilali:

> He possesses great veracity and honesty. He is a strict Mahometan; abstains from spirituous liquors and keeps the various fasts, particularly that of the Rhamadan [sic]. He is singularly exempt from all feeling of superstition; and holds in great contempt, the African beliefs in fetishes and evil spirits. He reads Arabic, and has a Koran (which however, I have not seen) in that language, but does not write it.[31]

This letter provides insights into Couper's views not only on Bilali but also of African Muslims. It highlights his diet, dress, and private life and challenges the notion that enslaved Africans were limited in their ability to read and write. According to Couper, "All children are taught to read and write Arabic by the priests they repeat the [verses] from the Koran, and write on a board, which when filled, is washed off."[32]

Bilali Mohammed was an enslaved Muslim who was owned by Thomas Spaulding, a friend of James Hamilton Couper who also had a plantation on St. Simons Island. Both Couper and Spaulding were part of the southern plantation elite society that deeply influenced the politics, culture, and economy of Georgia and the American South. Mohammed himself recorded the events of plantation life in Arabic, not his native tongue but a language he learned through Islamic schools in West Africa. Couper's grandson recounted in 1910 that Bilali "faced the East and called upon Allah" during his prayers.[33] Bilali also wrote a thirteen-page manuscript in Arabic that served as an Islamic devotional manual on spirituality, worship, and jurisprudence and were most likely extracts from the *Risalah*, one of the key texts used under the Maliki School of Islamic jurisprudence.

Bilali Mohammed's daily life on Sea Island in Georgia represents a continuity of traditions passed along from West Africa into the American South, traditions that also influenced the modern-day Gullah/Geechee and African American traditions. In 1829, Zephaniah Kingsley, a Southern plantation owner, wrote about Bilali Mohammed and Salih Bilali as having been influential in protecting their owners' interests during the War of 1812. He described them as "remarkable" and said that the two men were "influential negroes" and "professors of the Mahmodean religion."[34] Also, in 1939, the Workers Project Administration, which was created under President Franklin Roosevelt's Federal Writers Project, conducted interviews that included detailed accounts of Bilali's wife and children, as well as their Gullah/Geechee local vernacular and Islamic religious practice.

These descriptive accounts into the rituals and traditions of Salih Bilali and Bilali Mohammed provide a rich account of the literacy and religious tolerance of these two men, as well as their intricate social networks and religious experiences. They also provide an example of white American aristocrats of the South documenting their personal and public communications with these men. According to Spaulding's grandson, there were many enslaved African Muslims in South Carolina and Georgia. He states, "Many fresh from the darkest Africa, some of Moorish or Arabian descent, devout Mussulmans [Muslims], who prayed to Allah in the morning, noon and evening; all loyal and devoted to their respective owners."[35]

The final part of this chapter takes a look at the emergence of proto-Islamic movements in America and their relation to the experiences of Islam in West Africa and the New World. The story of Edward Wilmot Blyden explains the synergy between the emergence of these two experiences of Islam and the paradox that lies within them.[36] Blyden was born in St. Thomas in the Virgin Islands in 1832. He had a keen, intellectual mind, and he was encouraged by a white minister to join the ministry. Through the advice of this minister, Blyden traveled to the United States in 1850 intending to enroll at Rutgers Theological College, but he was turned down by the college.[37] Seven months later, Blyden departed from the United States to Monrovia, Liberia, at the invitation of the American Colonization Society (ACS). By the year 1858, Blyden had become a Presbyterian minister and was fulfilling the mission and direction of the ACS. During his time in Liberia, he moved quickly through the ranks and earned the titles of president of Liberia College and secretary of state of Liberia. He traveled to both Syria and Egypt for Arabic language cultivation. It is Blyden's argument that underlines the African / African in America Muslim slave perspective:

> The Mohammedan Negro is a much better Mohammedan than the Christian Negro is a Christian, because the Muslim Negro, as a learner, is a disciple, not an imitator. A disciple, when freed from leading-strings, may become a producer; an imitator never rises above a mere copyist. With a disciple progress is from within; imitator grows by accretion from without. The learning acquired by the disciple gives him capacity; that gained by an imitator terminates in itself. The one becomes a capable man; the other is a mere socialist. This explains the difference between the Mohammedan and the Christian Negro.[38]

I argue that Blyden was seeking to find a voice in understanding what religion and civilization had meant within the African context. He had made the journey out of his homeland in the Caribbean and had faced the racial hatred of America, and therefore, he was not oblivious to the intricacies of race, religion, and dominance. Blyden and other black intellectuals of the nineteenth century were impacted greatly by the racial stratifications in which they lived, and despite their newfound religious zeal, they were deeply reminded of the importance of their role in society and the subjugation they faced because of racial divisions. Blyden, himself, observed how Islam intersected with native African populations, stating that "Islamization in Africa didn't mean Arabization. Mohammedan conquests mean subjugation to the Koran and not to Arab or Turk."[39] Furthermore, he writes:

> Their local customs were not destroyed by the Arab influence introduced. They only assumed new forms, and adapted themselves to the new teachings. In all thriving communicates in West and Central Africa, it may be noticed that the Arab superstructure has been superimposed on a permanent indigenous substructure; so that what really took place when the Arab met the Negro in his own home, was a healthy amalgamation, and not an absorption or an undue repression.[40]

Many scholars have debated whether Blyden was a Muslim; some scholars, such as the Moroccan Muslim scholar Lotfi, argued in the affirmative, while others disagreed. In fact, Blyden may have been similar to enslaved African Muslims who had been forced to show publicly that they were Christians but were still privately Muslims. In other words, he might have been practicing *Taqiyyah* like the enslaved African Muslims in the United States who were well versed in this tradition.[41] Overall, Blyden clearly had a critical but deep appreciation for Islam, and he was fascinated yet deeply perplexed by the world, especially since he could not avoid his own African ancestry or the role of religion in it as he traveled. This was most evident in his efforts to fulfill his role as a Christian pastor and a spreader of Christianity. His earliest attitudes toward Islam, like those of many of his contemporaries, were largely shaped by European Orientalism. In his book *From West Africa to Palestine,* it is evident that his stay in Lebanon in 1866 was almost entirely with Europeans and Americans, including Dr. Daniel Bliss, president of the Syrian Protestant College.[42] Furthermore, during his travels throughout the Middle East, he interacted predominantly with Western Orientalists, rather than native inhabitants, thus pointing to a very narrow and limited interpretation of Islam. Despite this fact, however, he had a relatively positive view of African historical accomplishments. Quoting the words of the famous Liberian poet Hillary Teage: while exploring the halls of the great Egyptian pyramids of Cheops, Blyden said that he

> [f]elt I had a peculiar "heritage in the Great Pyramid." ... The blood seemed to flow faster through my veins. I seemed to hear the echo of those illustrious Africans ... I felt lifted out of the commonplace grandeur of modern times; and, could my voice have reached every African in the world, I would have earnestly addressed him in the language of Hilary Teage—Retake your fame.[43]

The historian Edward Curtis IV argues that in order for Blyden to make the linkages between his trip to Egypt and his own African nationalism, he engraved the word "Liberia" into the walls of the ancient tomb on July 11, 1866. Perhaps it was his desire to slowly connect his work in West Africa with the larger purpose of finding balance in his appreciation of the societies that he was closely understanding as his own. For Blyden, learning Arabic, living in West Africa, and being a Christian missionary had to have involved somewhat of an internal struggle. He must have experienced some culture shock as he came from the Caribbean and was confronted, via the visual and religious aesthetic of Muslim daily life, with a new religious faith of which he had not previously been very aware. In the January 1871 edition of the *Methodist Quarterly Review*, Blyden argues that Islam came to West Africa by the pen, not the sword, and that it encouraged deep learning, intellectual acumen, and discipline among its adherents. He writes, "Mohammedanism could easily be displaced by Christian influence, if Christian organizations would enter with vigor into this field."[44] Through the example of Blyden and his passion to connect Africa, Islam, and the New World, we also see the emergence of a *nouveau Islamique* developing in America. In his writings and lectures, he introduces students of Islamic, African, and American history to the shift from the old-world Islam of the enslaved Africans into American Islam by using the tool of Pan-Africanism, which would come to serve as the ideological connection for Islam in the United States.[45]

EMERGENCE OF EARLY AMERICAN ISLAMIC MOVEMENTS

As a result of the experience of the transatlantic slave trade and the institution of slavery, there has been considerable debate among scholars concerning the linkages between the Islam of the enslaved African Muslim populations and Black American Islam. For the purposes of this research, I focus and build upon the intellectual works of Dr. Sulayman Nyang, an esteemed professor of African studies at Howard University, who refers to "the sixty-year gap between African Muslim slaves and the African American Muslims of this century."[46] Though there is a considerable body of scholarly research about the legacy of enslaved African Muslims as they journeyed to the New World, this legacy was, in many ways, cut off from its original African-based forms.

This separation between the two communities, one having been rooted on the African continent with centuries of Islamic rituals and traditions and the other having emerged out of the Atlantic slave trade by initial appearance, seems openly very different. As a result of this unique geographical, cultural, and social separation, new adaptations were created in America. We argue that without the experiences of American slavery, the reconstruction period in the United States with its Jim Crow laws that contributed to the subjugation of people of African descent, and, most important, the emergence of proto-Islamic movements in America, the American Muslim community, which has been led largely by immigrant and white American Muslim leadership, would not be what it is today.

Blyden argues that through its intersection with African nationalism, Islam could serve a particular purpose. Blyden did not see Islam as claiming exceptionalism over the other Abrahamic faiths; in fact, he saw it as part of a continuum of shared views with Judaism and Christianity. This compelling point uniquely addresses how early Black American converts to Islam were able to harness their Islamic spiritual tradition via their personal Black American experience. It should be noted that this ability to utilize pre-Islamic cultural tradition and fuse it with one's current condition is a common theme that is seen throughout early Islamic movements. In the academic community today, there are serious concerns about how Black American Islam has been addressed. Notable scholars, including Yvonne Haddad, John Esposito, Stephen Barboza, Paul Barrrett, Aminah Beverly McCloud, and Kambiz GhaneaBassiri, all who have been referenced earlier, have provided interesting and unique insights into the contributions of Muslims in America.

However, Black American Muslims, despite being considered one of the oldest American Muslim communities, have witnessed the marginalization and possibly even the intentional erasure of their experiences and stories from normative Islamic traditions. Despite the role of Black American Islamic communities as the inheritors of a triple heritage of African, Islamic, and Western identity, scholars often miss the complexities of the Black American experience with Islam, and as a result, we have seen inaccurate assertions that are not rooted in an evidence- or empirical-based approach to this scholarship.[47] GhaneaBassiri amplifies this point by arguing that American Muslims have actively participated in American history and that black American Muslims, in particular, have been a critical voice in response to the peculiar political events and unique environment in the United States.[48]

Outside of the enslaved African Muslim experience, very few studies on the Black American Islamic experience have existed in the academic community prior to the late 1990s. Of all the cited studies on early Islamic movements that emerged out of the Black American Islamic experience, C. Eric Lincoln's *Black Muslims in America* stands out as the most authoritative analysis of the Nation of Islam. Alex Haley's *Malcolm X*, which has been translated into numerous foreign languages throughout the Middle East, Africa, Latin America, and Europe, provides deep insight into the conversion process of American Muslims.

In regards to the existence of Islam in modern-day America, religious movements like the Nation of Islam, as well as precursor organizations like the Moorish Science Temple and the Ahmadiyya movement, served as the foundation for its establishment. It is the argument of this work that without these movements, which uniquely addressed the specific circumstances of Black Americans who were deeply affected by institutionalized racism in America, the American Muslim community would not exist as it does today. All of today's Muslim Americans have benefitted from the hard work of Black American syncretic and Islamic movements. These movements were direct catalysts for the designers and organizers of large-scale American Muslim organizations such as the Islamic Society of North America (ISNA), Zaytuna College (the first accredited Muslim liberal arts college in the United States), and the Council of American Islamic Relations (CAIR). Despite what we characterize as selective decisions by these mainstream organizations to pick and choose the good and bad of the American Muslim community as they see fit, organizations and movements like the Nation of Islam and Ahmadiyya were the direct founders of Islam in America. Without these American groups, we would not have the modern-day institutions that have afforded immigrant Muslims the ability to freely express themselves in contemporary America. There are actually several movements that played a critical role in the development of Islam in America. During the period of Antebellum slavery and the subsequent generations up until the 1980s, the Black American Muslim community was given the ability to define Islam unilaterally without foreign interference or opposition and to create the foundation of North American forms of Islam, namely through Ahmadiyya missionaries, the Moorish Science Temple, the Nation of Islam, and the community associated with the late Imam W.D. Mohammed. Through this independence and ability to creatively take on their role as heirs of American Islam, the men and women affiliated with these groups created a practical and socially reforming movement that would leave lasting impressions on Black American and mainstream American culture. Only in the late 1970s and early

1980s did we see a gradual shift toward foreign influence, involving predominantly Wahhabi literalist and puritanical interpretations, on the Black American Muslim and the greater Muslim American communities. This influence has continued to have devastating consequences into the present day. The following sections discuss several of these early American Islamic movements.

AHMADIYYA MOVEMENT

The Ahmadiyya movement in the United States was an Islamic missionary movement that originated in Southeast Asia. Its ideological teachings were similar to those of mainstream Muslims as they were based on following the Qur'an and the example of Muhammad, the prophet of Islam. It departed from mainstream Islam, however, in the specific teachings of its founder, Hazrat Ghulam Ahmad, who, in 1888, declared himself the *Mahdi,* or promised Messiah in Islam and Christianity, and also argued that he was the incarnation of the Hindu god Krishna.[49] As we have seen in various Islamic revivalist movements in West Africa, Ahmad believed that Islam's beliefs and practices had been corrupted by Islamic scholars, and therefore, there was a need for a revival of Islam through high ethical, moral, and nonviolent actions. This theme of Islamic revivalism has been prevalent throughout Islamic history, and it was carried forward to America by Ahmadiyya missionaries who tailored their Islamic reformation into the American context. Mufti Muhammad Sadiq was an Ahmadiyya religious operative who was sent to the United States to spread the teachings of Islam, in general, and Ahmadiyya Islamic revivalism, specifically. According to numerous primary records of the Ahmadiyya, Sadiq was sent initially on a mission to recruit white Americans to Islam, but he quickly realized the challenges of racial identity in America after being detained at the airport upon entry for being a Muslim. Sadiq then adjusted his tactical approach to focus on Black Americans, who were subjected to clear and open racial abuse and who were likely to be more open to a universal racial, spiritual, and religious message that included them. By the time of Sadiq's arrival in the United States, many Black Americans had already become acquainted with Islam through the Pan-African philosophy of Marcus Garvey and his Universal Negro Improvement Association (UNIA).

Prior to the 1940s, Ahmadis originating from Southeast Asia were the primary propagators of mainstream Islam to Black American Muslims, and their purposeful decision to build their mosques in urban locations made it possible for many Black Americans to be exposed to normative Islamic teachings.[50] The Ahmadiyya movement is perhaps the single most important Islamic movement of the twentieth century for establishing Islam as an institution in America. Furthermore, Sylvia Chan-Malik at Rutgers University argues that, even within academic scholarship, there is prevalence to label the Ahmadiyya and other early Islamic movements as being part of proto-Islamic expression.[51] Using this theme, however, many of these early Islamic movements have been relegated to being unauthentic and as a result, scholars of Islamic and religious studies have generally dismissed their contributions to American Islam. By recognizing the Ahmadiyya movement as having been critical in the establishment of Islam in America, one is able to see how diverse forms of Islam spread and adapted to new frontiers. The Ahmadiyya influence is evident in the abundance of jazz musicians who were direct converts to Ahmadiyya Islamic teachings, including Yusuf Lateef, Ahmad Jamal, Art Blakey, and McCoy Turner.[52] As Fatima Fanusie argues in her work on Fard Muhammad, the Ahmadiyya message had been uniquely purposeful and strategic in order to gain a footing in the United States.[53] The Ahmadiyya legacy will eternally be remembered for their establishment of the *Moslem Sunrise*, a quarterly newspaper that continues to be the earliest and longest running Islamic magazine in the United States.

Despite having one of the most important movements in the establishment of early Islamic identity in America, the Ahmadiyya influence began to subside by the late 1920s and early 1930s. Most scholars argue that competing ideological directions were likely the cause of this decline. The increasing influence of Black Americans as a whole, including their having become more aggressive in their demands for equal rights in work, pay, education, and housing and the growth of the black empowerment movement, also played a significant role in the Ahmadiyya influence. In addition, increased tensions between Ahmadiyya missionaries in America and their Southasia-based religious leaders caused considerable tension, and as anxiety increased, Black Americans began to push against foreign influence and authority. These elements of and encounters with foreign versions of Islam, though helpful in exposing Black Americans to Islamic orthodoxy in various forms, were, in fact, contributing factors toward the movement by Black American Muslims to assert their own agency and identity as separate from non-American interpretations of Islamic thought. This is evident in the examples of both the Moorish Science Temple and the Nation of Islam.[54]

EARLY ISLAMIC MOVEMENTS AND THE QUR'AN

To understand the growing influence of Islam among Black Americans, one must first understand the migration of Black Americans to major cities along the East Coast and throughout the country in order to find employment and escape the Jim Crow laws of the American South. It was also during the 1920s and 1930s that a new multireligious, spiritual, and eclectic zeal was sweeping over the United States. This zeal, having largely taken root in white America, involved religious revivalist movements, such as the Theosophical Society, Christian Science, Mormonism, and Shakerism.[55] These spiritual wars that were sweeping across America were not anything new. Even in the 1800s, the word "spirituality," defined as a quest to understand the purpose of life through nonorganized religious experience outside the normative Christian experience, had developed a slow and steady group of admirers. Writers Walt Whitman and Ralph Waldo Emerson were just two examples of Americans who largely categorized themselves as wayfarers seeking to understand the supernatural and metaphysical aspects of life with all of its complexities. In his 1871 work *Democratic Vistas*, Whitman wrote:

> And is a result that no organization or church can ever achieve. . . . I should say, indeed, that only in the perfect contamination and solitariness of individuality may the spirituality of religion come forth at all. Only here, and on such terms, the mediation, the devout, ecstasy, the soaring flight.[56]

Whitman was seeking to understand the growing shift of this century toward a personalized and individualized connection to the divine based on finding a purpose beyond organized religion. Furthermore, Dr. Leigh E. Schmidt, a professor of religion at Princeton University, describes in his book *Restless Souls: The Making of American Spirituality* certain defining characteristics of American spirituality in the tradition of Emerson and Whitman. He highlights the following characteristics: (1) a yearning for mystical experience or epiphany awareness; (2) valuing silence, solitude, and sustained meditation; (3) a belief in the immanence of the divine in nature and attunement to that presence; (4) a cosmopolitan appreciation of religious variety, along with the search for unity in diversity; (5) an ethical earnestness in pursuit of justice-producing, progressive reforms; and (6) an emphasis on self-cultivation, artistic creativity, and adventuresome seeking.[57] This search for meaning and self-critique among early American philosophers, thinkers, and dreamers was not based solely on transporting oneself to the supernatural but also on a work ethic of actual meaningful application. As a result, the Black American encounter with new financial resources as well as the safety and freedom to express themselves more openly should also be seen as part of a larger story that other Americans were confronting and addressing as well. As such, Black American institutions were gradually able to articulate how their personal spiritual and religious experiences were different from the mainstream church experiences of the past. As mentioned earlier, Black Americans' quest to learn more about themselves and find an identity was more evident in the cosmopolitan urban centers. Thus, the early Islamic movements in America must be seen within the broader scope of descendants of enslaved Africans yearning for and seeking practical, personal, and longer-term spiritual guidance that could provide them with meaning, purpose, and memory in their lives.

For the purposes of this book, the following organizations are arguably the single most important organizations to establish Islam in America and their recruitment of Black Americans to Islam as articulated by their interpretation.

MOORISH SCIENCE TEMPLE

The Moorish Science Temple was established by Timothy Drew (1886–1929), a leading Pan-Africanist who became a key influencer of numerous Black American early Islamic movements in America. Drew traced his ideological roots to Marcus Garvey and would later adopt the name Noble Drew Ali. He appropriated into his deeply esoteric organizational doctrine Islamic religious motifs; elements of freemasonry, theosophy, and Pan-Africanism; and symbols from the modern Middle East. Drew also borrowed from a number of other ideas in an attempt to find an identity for his group. At its peak, his movement included around thirty thousand members, quite an accomplishment for a newfound social, political, and religious movement in the context of the times and the extreme poverty and limited public transportation of the communities it influenced. Drew established religious centers in Detroit and Lansing, Michigan; Pittsburgh and Philadelphia, Pennsylvania; Chicago, Illinois; Milwaukee, Wisconsin; Cleveland and Youngstown, Ohio; Charleston, West Virginia; Richmond and Petersburg, Virginia; Pine Bluff, Arkansas; and Baltimore, Maryland.[58] After years of internal rivalry, Drew established a permanent headquarters in Chicago in 1923 and named his movement the Moorish Holy Temple of Science, later changing the name to the Moorish Science Temple of America.[59]

The early Islamic movements in America had identity at the core of their influence, and for Drew, the aim of the Moorish Temple was to impress upon its followers the importance of dignity, self-respect, and responsibility. According to followers' archival narratives, they were to be known as Asiatic or Moorish people from Morocco. This lore, which was created by Drew largely without the use of any documented records proving their ancestral links to Morocco, sought to bring some dignity to the Black American who was subjected to discrimination, poverty, and unfair racial treatment.

By creating a myth as well as using some factual historical accounts, Drew sought to create a message that resonated with disaffected and downtrodden Black Americans who sought to reclaim their purpose and self-worth. In one of Drew's teachings, he called himself "the prophet" whose job was to "lift the fallen Asiatic nation of North America by teaching its members their true religion (Islam), their true nationality (Moorish) and their true genealogy, which he taught could be traced directly to Jesus, who was a descendant of the ancient Canaanites, the Moabites and the inhabitants of Africa."[60] By giving Black Americans these self-empowerment themes, Drew facilitated a massive resurrection of those individuals who were gradually finding techniques to address their condition in America. By donning fezzes, establishing lodges with Arab-Islamic names, and appropriating the Islamic crescent and star in the organizational cultural dress, Drew slowly introduced into urban culture what ultimately became a popular Black American Muslim tradition for generations to come. While it is evident that Drew had no direct connections to the ritualistic religious traditions of Islam in West Africa, he nevertheless facilitated the development of a new way of imagination for the Black American community by introducing them to various aspects of Islamic practices.

Finally, as I will continue to highlight with other early Islamic movements, the overlapping thread of these groups lies in their ability to point to the Qur'an and normative Islamic teachings as a source of idealism, while at the same time adapting certain aspects of traditional Islam to serve the purpose of supporting their fight against the plight of Black Americans. The Islamic idealism of many early Black American Islamic movements is hardly coincidental. Instead, it can be seen as relating back to US relations with Morocco, which is documented as having been the first country (debated between France as well) to have recognized the United States as an independent nation. On June 23, 1786, Morocco signed a treaty of peace and friendship with the United States, thus beginning the process of an enduring, formalized, and long-standing relationship between the two countries.[61] In 1790, the South Carolina House of Representatives passed the Moors Sundry Act, which provided clarity on the status of free individuals for the sultan of Morocco, Mohammed Ben Abdallah. The resolution stated that free citizens of Morocco were not subject to the same laws as American slaves and blacks. Because of this peace treaty, four individuals petitioned the South Carolina legislature, claiming that they were free subjects of the Moroccan ruler and should not be tried (as scheduled) under the Negro Act of 1740.[62] This is but one example of Morocco's influence on the Moorish Science Temple and its desire to connect with the larger Islamic world.

In 1927, Drew wrote his own version of the Qur'an, called the *Holy Koran* (also called the *Circle Seven Koran*). He prepared several iterations of this sixty-four-page book and primarily used four major texts as his reference: the Qur'an, the Bible, *The Aquarian Gospels of Jesus Christ* (an occult version of the New Testament), and *Unto Thee I Grant* (literature of the Rosicrucian Brotherhood). According to Richard Brent Turner, Sufism likely influenced Drew as well, particularly the teachings of Hazrat Inayat Khan, an Indian mystic who preached a form of Sufism that taught universalism and the common values of all religions. Drew's philosophical teachings embraced similar ideas of love, truth, peace, and freedom and borrowed from many religions and cultures, as did Khan's.[63] Drew, like the leaders of other early Islamic communities, sought to reform Black Americans' condition from marginalization by reconstructing their identity to one that was built on the enslaved African Muslim legacy and a broader Pan-Islamic connection. Drew, like Elijah Muhammad, presented Christianity as an inferior religion that oppressed Blacks and provided a meticulous theological plan to support his argument. Turner writes that Drew created new identities for his members by saying the following:

> When Noble Drew Ali said, "The Name means everything," he was convinced that he could change the political and economic fate of African Americans in the Jim Crow era by ethnicizing the name of the race and by changing the names of the followers, thereby erasing the stigma of slavery and distancing them from ordinary Negroes who were not respected as Americans. The ultimate objective . . . was to erase the stigma of their minority group status in order to be accepted as genuine Americans by the prevailing culture.[64]

Drew's movement provided the building blocks for thousands of Black Americans' introduction to Islam in the early twentieth century. The Moorish Science Temple was an essential component of the development of the Nation of Islam's ascendency and the massive conversion of Black Americans to Islam. In the words of Lincoln, "It was not Islam, but it was a significant recovery of the awareness of Islam."[65]

MARCUS GARVEY AND THE UNIA

Outside of the Ahmadiyya movement, there was, perhaps, no other movement that brought together Islam and Pan-Africanism in America as much as the Universal Negro Improvement Association (UNIA). This organization, created by Marcus Garvey, had chapters in forty nations on several continents and became the vanguard of black pride and self-independence.[66] The Garvey movement promoted a universal teaching for all people of African descent, regardless of faith, and was, thus, attractive to early Black American Islamic movements. Both Noble Drew Ali, the founder of the Moorish Science Temple, and Elijah Muhammad, the leader of the Nation of Islam, were directly impacted by the teachings of Garvey and frequently referenced his work in their public speeches. Although Garvey and many members of the UNIA were Christian, the UNIA fully embraced religious differences. Garvey himself was a student of world religion and, therefore, very familiar with Islam. Garvey was introduced to Islam in 1912 by Duse Muhammad Ali, a Sudanese Egyptian Pan-Africanist who later became minister of African Affairs for the UNIA. During his travels throughout the United States in 1925,

Duse Ali gave a number of public and private speeches and was integral in encouraging a significant number of practicing Black American Muslims to join the UNIA.[67]

Movements like the UNIA provided the philosophical and practical experience for Black Americans to instill in themselves a sense of pride and dignity. In a society where people of African descent were struggling with limited economic opportunities and continued racial suppression, movements like the UNIA aided communities and individuals alike in addressing their conditions. Professor E.U. Essien-Udom, in his book *Black Nationalism: The Search for an Identity*, writes:

> The tragedy of the Negro in America is that he has rejected his origins—the essentially human meaning implicit in the heritage of slavery, prolonged suffering and social rejection. By rejecting this unique group experience and favoring assimilation and even biological amalgamation, he thus denies himself the creative possibilities inherent in it and in his folk culture. This "dilemma" is fundamental; it severely limits his ability to evolve a new identity or a meaningful synthesis, capable of endowing his life with meaning and purpose.[68]

This illustration by Essien-Udom captures the plight of Black American life and is central to understanding the existence and, ultimately, the struggle to raise the consciousness of Black American men and women. It is largely through these early Black empowerment and Black American Islamic movements that Black Americans were able to directly address this struggle. This point is driven home even further by W. E. B. Dubois in his book *The Souls of Black Folk*, in which he eloquently captures the Black American experience. He writes:

> The Negro is a sort of seventh son, born with a veil, and gifted with second-sight in this American world—a world which yields him no true self-consciousness, but only lets him see himself through the revelation of the outer world. It is a peculiar sensation, this double consciousness, this sense of always looking at one's self through the eyes of others, of measuring one's soul by the tape of a world that looks on in amused contempt and pity.

And further laments:

> The history of the American Negro is the history of this strife—this longing to attain self-conscious manhood, to merge his double self into a better and truer self. In this merging he wishes neither of the older selves to be lost. He would not Africanize America, for America has too much to teach the world and Africa. He would not bleach his Negro soul in a flood for white Americanism, for he knows that Negro blood has a message for the world. He simply wishes to make it possible for a man to be both a Negro and an American, without

being cursed and spit upon by his fellows without having the doors of Opportunity closed roughly in his face.[69]

From this experience captured by Dubois, one gains a further insight into the challenge of Black American identity, consciousness, and self-awareness. In many ways, the UNIA, the Ahmadiyya movement, and the Nation of Islam movement became the building blocks to address Black identity in America.

NATION OF ISLAM

The Nation of Islam was an indigenous Black American movement established by Wali Fard Muhammad and implemented by Elijah Muhammad. This movement combined elements of freemasonry, spirituality, mythology, Black Nationalism, and made-up theology to address the conditions and circumstances of life for Black Americans. It directly critiqued white America for its marginalizing racial injustices toward Black Americans. Elijah Muhammad, through careful instructions from Fard Muhammad, instituted a step-by-step program to radically reform the mental, physical, and economic state of Black Americans. C. Eric Lincoln describes Elijah Muhammad's task as a rather Herculean effort to reform the condition of his people:

> The complexity of Mr. Muhammad's task was beyond imagination, for as Messenger of Allah he had committed himself to nothing less than the restoration of the most despised and brutalized segment of American Christianity back to a level of dignity and self-appreciation from which informed choices could be made. . . . His initial "parish" was the slums of the Black ghettos of the industrial cities, and his potential converts were the slum created outcasts of a developing technocratic society. His people were those who were the most battered by racism and stifled by convention, and whose experience of the white man's invincibility made the appearance of Black inferiority seem as reasonable as it was pervasive.[70]

As a whole, the Nation of Islam was a social reform movement focused on the experience of Black American life. Its agenda included a moral and physical code in which adherents were instructed to abide by strict measures of discipline, including abstinence from alcohol, gambling, fornication, adultery, drugs, and dancing, as well as dietary restrictions, such as avoidance of pork. These and other rules were carefully orchestrated so as to make clear the divisions between members and nonmembers of the Nation of Islam.

Many Black Americans were sympathetic toward the Nation of Islam and saw the techniques it employed as vital. It likely had millions of followers in its height. However, many Black Americans were hesitant to join this new movement that articulated new language and messages and were often quite critical of the white American establishment. Though this research doesn't address the minutiae of doctrinal details on the Nation of Islam or other early Islamic movements, we do attempt to describe the Nation of Islam and other such movements as having offered elements of Islamic reform to address the physical, emotional, and spiritual conditions of its followers. Furthermore, it argues that, since their inceptions, early Black American Islamic movements directly utilized authoritative Islamic religious texts, including the Qur'an, while also employing strategic techniques such as mythmaking in an effort to change the condition of men and women who were suffering from the legacy of centuries of physical and emotional abuse.

While many scholars of Islamic and Middle Eastern studies relegate the Nation of Islam and other early Islamic movements to the status of "heterodox" or "proto-Islamic," I choose not to use this language. Instead, I seek to build on the work of Dr. Ernest Allen, a University of Massachusetts professor specializing in Black American Muslims who rejects the notion that the Moorish Science Temple and the Nation of Islam should be placed in these categories. According to Allen, these categories are largely defined by scholars of Islam who are not familiar with the Black American Islamic experience. Instead, he characterizes these groups as syncretic and describes them as being no different from other denominations of established religious communities that select and borrow the ideological perspectives and traditions that suit them best.[71] As noted in previous chapters, this understanding fits well with the explanation as to how Islam acculturated itself in West Africa.

This theme, discussed by Allen and other academics, helps explain why Black American Islam has often been viewed as subordinate to other Islamic perspectives by the largely immigrant-based American Muslim population and overseas Muslims who have largely dominated the discourse. The Nation of Islam's teachings, like those of its ideological predecessors, were against the views imposed on them by white Americans. By introducing new verbiage into its lexicon, such as "Asiatic" and "Black is beautiful," the Nation of Islam was building on the ideological views of its predecessors, including the Ahamadiyya movement, the UNIA, and the Moorish Science Temple. However, the Nation of Islam went a step further, not only rejecting the white racist teachings about Black Americans and the idea of inferiority but also providing an alternative master narrative for their followers. By using an inversion process highlighting that blacks were good, beautiful, and even gods, they directly critiqued mainstream white American society and the current condition of inferiority in which Black Americans found themselves. Lincoln describes Elijah Muhammad's effort to address this condition in the following terms:

> The complexity of Mr. Muhammad's task was beyond imagination, for as Messenger of Allah he had committed himself to nothing less than the restoration of the most despised and brutalized segment of American Christianity

back to a level of dignity and self-appreciation from which informed choices could be made. ... His initial "parish" was the slums of the Black ghettos of the industrial cities, and his potential converts were the slum-created outcasts of a developing technocratic society. His people were those who were the most battered by racism and stifled by convention, and who's [sic] experience of the white man's invincibility made the acceptance of Black inferiority seem as reasonable as it was pervasive.[72]

Elijah Muhammad faced considerable pushback on his newfound teachings and was often confronted by hostile elements from within the government at local, state, and federal levels. Even within the black community, Black American intellectuals were highly critical of his movement and its teachings and ridiculed it on a continuous basis. Like the doctrines of the other early Islamic movements, Elijah Muhammad's fused mythology together with theology from a number of primary sources. For the Nation of Islam and the Moorish Science Temple, the connections between African heritage, spirituality, Black Nationalism, orthodox Islam, and, in some instances, a mythical understanding of Islam, allowed them to directly describe their experiences on their own terms. As argued first by Joseph R. Washington Jr. in his book *Black Religion: The Negro and Christianity in the United States*, "Independent Negro (Christian) congregations and institutions are ineffective among Negros's because they failed in faithfulness to Black religion."[73] Reinhold Niebuhr also states, "Contending factions in a social struggle require morale and morale is created by the right dogmas, symbols and emotionally potent oversimplifications."[74] Sherman Jackson, at the University of Southern California, argues that "black religion for its part has always been rich in powerful oversimplifications and its rejectionist's instinct has always served to insulate it from the anesthetizing forces of accommodationalism, domestication, and intellectualism, all of which tend to mollify rather than address the demand for change."[75] The fact that the Nation of Islam, the Moorish Science Temple, and the UNIA would use their American religious experience and their syncretic version of Islam as a form of holy protest and critique of the white establishment allowed them to directly engage the space of resistance against that establishment. Furthermore, by utilizing a version of Islamic ideals, they created legitimacy for their argument using their own terms and conditions.

Through their high visibility, strong family work ethic, strong emphases on education and self-improvement, and nationwide network of religious centers and worship sites, the Nation of Islam introduced in mass scale what it was to be a Muslim in America.[76] Through their weekly newspaper, *Muhammad Speaks*; their rejection of pork and drugs; and their antiviolence campaign, the Nation of Islam introduced a reform movement in America that hit at the core of economic, political, and social life in the Black American urban community. The Nation of Islam's teachings, which provided the backdrop for the popularization of Islam in mainstream American culture, also facilitated a broader Muslim internationalism.

One of the leading voices of the Nation of Islam was Malcolm X, also known as El Hajj Malik Al Shabazz. His influence, I argue, facilitated a stronger connection between the Nation of Islam and the broader Islamic world, one that went beyond the imagined ideal or mythical interpretation as demonstrated by the Moorish Science Temple and the early days of the Nation of Islam.[77] Malcolm saw the Black American struggle as part of a broader, global battle of Third World people against foreign domination, imperialism, and colonialism.[78] The Nation of Islam finally acquired its long-sought identity by connecting Malcolm with its larger struggle for freedom for black Americans in America.

Many scholars have denied the Nation of Islam's influence on Malcolm's life and have instead given credit to his reawakening when he went on the pilgrimage to Mecca. Dr. Sohail Daultazai, in his book *Black Star, Crescent Moon*, argues that the Nation of Islam was the impetus for Malcolm's ascendancy. Daulatzai further argues that Malcolm's first trips to Africa and the Arab world were in 1959 in which he was deeply affected by the assassination of Patrice Lumumba, met with Fidel Castro in Harlem, vocally supported the Mau Mau rebellion in Kenya, supported Nasser in Egypt, allied with the Vietnamese victory of Dien Bien Phu, and attended the Bandung Conference in 1955, all while he was a member of the Nation of Islam.[79] This goes against the general belief that the Nation of Islam was not addressing overseas issues. The inheritors of the early Islamic movements and the Nation of Islam can learn from the truly cosmopolitan and international nature of these communities.[80]

As C. Eric Lincoln states,

> Elijah Muhammad must be credited with the serious reintroduction of Islam to the United States in modern times, giving it the peculiar mystique, the appeal, and the rest without which it could not have penetrated the bastion of Judea-Christian democracy. If now, as it appears the religion of Islam has a solid foothold and an indeterminate future in North America, it is Elijah Muhammad alone to whom initial credit must be given.[81]

The Nation of Islam in general, and Elijah Muhammad in particular, offered a fusion of traditional Islam, mythology, and alternative theological narratives to address the social experience of black American life. As will be further outlined in the next chapter, which focuses on the role, evolution, and contribution of the late Imam W.D. Mohammed, W.D. Mohammed not only carried forward the initial groundwork of his father's teachings but also brought about a radical transformation by instituting Islamic "Sunni" orthodoxy and doing so on the terms of Black American Muslims.[82] What we will see from the efforts of W.D. Mohammed, which I argue were a continuum of the good practices of social dignity and black consciousness encouraged by his father but also a rejection of the divisive teachings of black supremacy and anti-Semitism, is an independent and direct critique on normative and traditional Islamic institutions, which overemphasize blind ritualism. He offered a direct challenge to the immigrant wave of 1952 and 1965, arguing that Black American Muslims could be both American and Muslim on their own terms and without foreign interference that imposed a cultural and dogmatic rigidness that was imported from immigrant home countries.

NOTES

1. Eric Williams, *Capitalism & Slavery* (Chapel Hill: University of North Carolina Press, 1994).
2. Sherman Pyatt and John Meffert, *Black America Series* (Charleston, SC: Arcadia Publishing, 2000).
3. Katia M. de Queiros Mattoso, *To Be a Slave in Brazil, 1550–1888*, trans. Arthur Goldhammer (New Brunswick and London: Rutgers University Press, 1994)
4. Mechal Sobel, *Traeblin' On: The Slave Journey to an Afro-Baptist Faith* (Westport, CT: Greenwood Press, 1979).
5. Phillip Curtin, *The Atlantic Slave Trade: A Census* (Madison: University of Wisconsin Press, 1969).
6. Peter Wood, *Black Majority: Negroes in Colonial South Carolina from 1670 through the Stono Rebellion* (London: WW Norton, 1974).
7. Ibid.
8. Daniel C. Littlefield, *Rice and Slaves: Ethnicity and the Slave Trade in Colonial South Carolina* (Baton Rouge, LA: LSU Press, 1981), 116.
9. Leo Weiner, *Africa and the Discovery of America* (Philadelphia: Innes and Sons, 1922).
10. Bilali Muhammad's daughters, mentioned by Georgia Writers' Project interviewees, were born in Africa and were transported to the United States by their parents.
11. Thomas Bluett, *Some Memories of the Life of Job, the Son of Solomon, the High Priest of Bonda in Africa* (London: Printed for Richard Ford, at the Angel in the Poultry, 1744).
12. Ibid.
13. Cyrus Griffin, "The Unfortunate Moor," *Natchez Southern Galaxy*, December 13, 1827. Reprinted in *African Muslims in Antebellum America: A Sourcebook*, edited by Allan Austin (London: Garland, 1984), 135.
14. GhaneaBassiri, *A History of Islam in America*, 21.
15. Raboteau, *Slave Religion*.
16. Robin Law and Paul E. Lovejoy, eds., *The Biography of Mahommah Gardo Baquaqua: His Passage from Slavery to Freedom in Africa and America* (Princeton, NJ: Markus Wiener Publishers, 2003), 92.
17. Halverson, "West African Islam in Colonial and Antebellum South Carolina."
18. L. D. Turner, *Africanisms in the Gullah Dialect* (Columbia: University of South Carolina Press, 2002).
19. Abdul-Qasim al-Qushayri, *Al-Qushayri's Epistle on Sufism*, trans. Alexander D. Knysh (Reading: Garnet Publishing, 2007), 336.
20. Allan D. Austin, *African Muslims in Antebellum America: A Sourcebook* (New York: Garland, 1995).
21. *Columbian Herald*, 1790, microfiche.
22. *Charleston Times*, November 17, 1903, microfiche.
23. Charles Ball, *Slavery in the United States: A Narrative of the Life and Adventures of Charles Ball* (New York: John S. Taylor, 1837), 165.
24. Halverson, "West African Islam in Colonial and Antebellum South Carolina."

25. Ibid., 167.
26. John B. O. Landurum, *History of Spartanburg County* (Atlanta: Franklin Printing and Publishing, 1900), 254.
27. Theodore Dwight, "Condition and Character of Negroes in Africa," *Methodist Quarterly Review* 46 (January 1864), 89.
28. Bluett, *Some Memories of the Life of Job*.
29. Terry Alford, *Prince among Slaves*, 30th anniversary ed. (New York: Oxford University Press, 2007); Allan D. Austin, *African Muslims in Antebellum America: Transatlantic Stories and Spiritual Struggles* (New York: Routledge, 1997).
30. Ibid., 15–57.
31. Ibid., 35–89
32. Ibid.
33. Ibid.
34. Ibid.
35. Ibid.
36. Edward E. Curtis IV, *Islam in Black America: Identitiy, Liberation, and Difference in African-American Islamic Thought* (Albany: State University of New York Press, 2002).
37. Sherman Jackson, *Islam and the Blackamerican: Looking toward the Third Resurrection* (London: Oxford University Press, 2005).
38. Edward W. Blyden, "The Call of Providence to the Descendants of Africa in America," in *Negro Social and Political Thought, 1850–1920*, ed. Howard Brotz (New York: Basic Books, 1966).
39. Edward W. Blyden, *Liberia's Offering* (New York: J. A. Gray, 1862).
40. Ibid., 14.
41. Samory Rashid, *Black Muslims in the US* (New York: Palgrave Macmillan, 2013).
42. Edward W. Blyden, *From West Africa to Palestine* (Manchester: John Heywood, 1873), 37–42, 159–62, 180.
43. Ibid., 104–5.
44. Edward W. Blyden, *Christianity, Islam and the Negro Race* (1887; reprint, Edinburgh: Edinburg University Press, 1967), 173–88.
45. Richard Brent Turner, *Islam in the African-American Experience* (Bloomington: Indiana University Press, 2003), 45–59.
46. Sulayman Nyang, *Islam in the United States of America* (Chicago: Kazi Publications, 1999).
47. Yvonne Yazbeck Haddad and John L. Esposito, eds., *Muslims on the Americanization Path?* (New York: Oxford University Press, 2000), 10.
48. Rashid, *Black Muslims in the US*.
49. Adil Hussain Khan, *From Sufism to Ahmadiyya: A Muslim Minority Movement in South Asia* (Bloomington: Indiana University Press, 2015).
50. Fatima Fanusie, "Fard Muhammad," PhD diss, Howard University, April 2008.
51. Sylvia Chan-Malik, "Profile: Black American Women in the Ahmadiyya Movement of Islam," *Sapelo Square*, accessed February 29, 2016, https://sapelosquare.com/2016/02/24/profile-black-american-women-in-the-ahmadiyya-movement-of-islam/.
52. Hisham Aidi, *Rebel Music: Race, Empire and the New Muslim Youth Culture* (New York: Pantheon Books, 2014); Robert Dannin, *Black Pilgrimage to Islam* (Oxford: Oxford University Press, 2002).
53. Fanusie, "Fard Muhammad."
54. Amaddou Shakur, 'Islam in America: The Middle Period (1900–1950)," *Islamic Horizons Magazine*, May/June 2016.
55. Hans A. Baer, *The Black Spiritual Movement: A Religious Response to Racism*, 2nd ed. (Knoxville: University of Tennessee Press, 2001).
56. Ibid.
57. Leigh Schmidt, *Restless Souls: The Making of American Spirituality* (Berkeley: University of California Press, 2005).
58. Turner, *Islam in the African-American Experience*.
59. Ibid.

60. Ibid.

61. "Treaty with Morocco June 28 and July 15, 1786," Avalon Project, accessed February 12, 2017, http://avalon.law.yale.edu/18th_century/bar1786t.asp.

62. *Charleston City Gazette*, January 28, 1790, and the *Charleston State Gazette of South Carolina*, February 1 and 4, 1790, microfiche.

63. Turner, *Islam in the African-American Experience*.

64. Gwendolyn Zoharah Simmons, "From Muslims in America to American Muslims," *Journal of Islamic Law and Culture* 10, no. 3 (2008): 254–80.

65. C. Eric Lincoln, "The Muslim Mission," *African American Religious Studies: An Interdisciplinary Anthology*, ed. Gayraud S. Wilmore (Durham, NC: Duke University Press, 1989), 345.

66. Ibid.

67. Ibid.

68. E. U. Essien-Udom, *Black Nationalism: The Search for an Identity* (Chicago: University of Chicago Press, 1995).

69. W. E. B. Dubois, *The Souls of Black Folk* (New York: Penguin Books, 1989).

70. Lincoln, *Black Muslims in America*.

71. Ernest Allen Jr. "Identity and Destiny: The Formative Views of the Moorish Science Temple and the Nation of Islam," in *Muslims on the Americanization Path?* Edited by Yvonne Haddad and John Esposito (New York: Oxford University Press, 2000), 243 n. 2.

72. Lincoln, *Black Muslims in America*, 346.

73. Joseph R. Washington Jr., *Black Religion: The Negro and Christianity in the United States* (Toronto: Reginald Saunders, 1964).

74. Ibid.

75. Jackson, *Islam and the Blackamerican*.

76. William H. Banks Jr., *The Black Muslims: African American Achievers* (Philadelphia: Chelsea House, 1997).

77. Magnus O. Bassey, *Malcolm X and African American Self-Consciousness* (Lewistown, NY: Edwin Mellen Press, 2005); Robert E. Terrill, *The Cambridge Companion to Malcolm X* (Cambridge: Cambridge University Press, 2010).

78. Partha Chatterjee, *Nationalist Thought and the Colonial World: A Derivative Discourse* (London: Zed Books, 1986).

79. Sohail Daulatzai, *Black Star, Crescent Moon: The Muslim International and Black Freedom Struggle beyond America* (Minneapolis: University of Minnesota Press, 2012).

80. James Jennings, ed., *Blacks, Latinos and Asians in Urban America: Status and Prospects for Politics and Activism* (London: Praeger, 1994); Yuri Kochiyama, *The Impact of Malcolm X on Asian-American Politics and Activism* (London: Praeger, 1994).

81. Lincoln, *Black Muslims in America*, 345.

82. I argue that W.D. Mohammed introduced normative Islam to his community, which can be characterized as "Sunni" Islam. But as you will see later, W.D. Mohammed offered new language and sought to depart from the labeling and staunch ritualism of the Muslim world, which, in his estimation, caused some of the problems of ethnic, racial, and intra-Muslim politics pervasive throughout the Islamic world.

Chapter Four

Imam W.D. Mohammed, the Patron Saint of American Islam

Personality, Intellectual Teachings, and Reformation

In the post-Enlightenment Western world, a large segment of the population has been influenced by Protestantism and the popularized "back to the Bible" attraction, which places the center of gravity of religion in the American context largely on a simplistic understanding of Judeo-Christian beliefs deduced from either the Bible or the Torah. Muslim communities in the West often follow a similar tendency, and as we look at Islam being introduced to Americans on a large scale, the Qur'an is presented as a religious text to complete the Abrahamic faith tradition in this practical form of religion. In the contemporary era, Islam has either been seen as an Eastern religion with violent tendencies and simply relegated to the status of the faith that caused the devastation on 9/11 or been viewed as an unknown faith that seems utterly foreign, immigrant, and "other" to ordinary America. As highlighted previously, Muslims have been in America since its inception, and, contrary to contemporary notions emphasizing the role of the immigrant Muslim population, it was enslaved African Muslims who were the first vanguards of establishing Islam in America in both the public and private discourse.

Imam Wallace Deen Mohammed (1933–2008), affectionately called W.D. Mohammed,[1] is a continuation of the legacy of the enslaved African Muslim experience and its encounter with American Protestantism, chattel slavery, Jim Crow laws of the American South, and the social experiment of Islam's encounter in the New World. W.D. Mohammed was the sociocultural religious leader of the largest unified American Muslim community in the Western Hemisphere in the twentieth century. With his followers (including those who currently follow his leadership even after his death) representing a quarter of the American Muslim population, W.D. Mohammed was able to usher in the largest mass communal conversion to mainstream Islam and introduce a gradual process of moving away from his father's divisive teachings of black nationalism and proto-Islamic concepts into universal Islamic values that filtered through the Black American experience.[2] For W.D. Mohammed, the aim was to indigenize mainstream Islamic beliefs and practices and recalibrate the old Nation of Islam teachings into mainstream Islamic beliefs. His desire was for an Islam that was distinctly Islamic yet proudly Black American, and he saw Black Americans "reverting" to the original religion of their African ancestors rather than converting to a new religion. W.D. Mohammed wrote:

> I believe firmly that Al-Islam is in America by Allah's Will to be our salvation and to establish African Americans. . . . If a child was taken from his parents by a kidnapper, and that parent was hurt and done a terrible injustice and so was the child; If no help comes to the child, and the parent also is being slandered and mistreated and lied against, then don't you know that if there is a God, that God should in time do something for that situation? The mercy and injustice would be to bring that child and that parent back together. Even if the parent is dead, if the child is still living, the justice would be to reconcile that child with its parents.
>
> But our parents are not dead; they are still alive. There are African Muslims still in Africa, and history reports that many of us were brought from African Muslims and were enslaved here in America. Slave traders (buyers) did not go to churches in Africa to get slaves for America. When I was following my father's teachings (the late Honorable Elijah Muhammad), I felt it strongly. I felt that Allah had plans for us. . . . It is not popular for an African American race to embrace the religion of a White race, when that religion is imaged in a "White man," the "word" and "God." The only way that could happen is that we were under them and could not express freedom of choice.[3]

BIOGRAPHY AND PERSONALITY

Born to Elijah Muhammad and Clara Muhammad on October 30, 1933, in Detroit, Michigan, W.D. Mohammed was raised in the home of the founder and leader of the social reform movement called the Nation of Islam. W.D. Mohammed took over the historical community of the Nation of Islam in 1975 and immediately brought its adherents into mainstream Sunni Islam.

This, in turn, brought about far-reaching social and doctrinal reforms that were previously practiced and instituted. Perhaps foreshadowing these changes in a rather predictive manner, Elijah Muhammad, in the Nation of Islam's foundational text, *Message to the Black Man,* devotes two entire chapters to "Islam" and "Prayer Service" that could easily be acceptable interpretations for mainstream Muslims throughout the world. He shares this information despite his incessant advocacy of Black supremacy and constant denigration of the white race,[4] thus suggesting that an approach to radically transform Black American life by fusing together religious and culturally appropriate themes that appealed to new recruits and followers of his movement was quite intentional. W.D. Mohammed himself eloquently captured this point in the following statement: "The Nation of Islam was a religion and social movement organization. In fact, the religion as it was introduced to the membership was more a social reform philosophy than Orthodox Islam."[5]

Even W. Fard Muhammad, often referred to as Professor Fard or Wali, who was the ideological teacher of the Nation of Islam and who established the movement in America, fused together traditional Islamic concepts, mythology, and later some black nationalism principles to lure in new members. Fard claimed that he had been born in Mecca on February 26, 1877, and created a belief that his light complexion, which indicated he was either from Southeast Asia or the Arab world, provided a sense of legitimacy for the message he was seeking to convey.

Furthermore, Fard claimed to be of royal ancestry, a son of a wealthy member of the tribe of Quraysh, the family and tribal affiliation of the Prophet Muhammad. Lastly, he described himself as having been trained as a diplomat and as working on behalf of the modern-day kingdom of Saudi Arabia.[6] All this sought to provide legitimacy to the new theology he was introducing into the Black American community and the alternative religious narrative that would come to play an effective role in the urban centers of America. Through his numerous public speeches, W.D. Mohammed described the purposeful strategy of Fard Muhammad and his disciples to use the power of myth as a tool to address the masses of disenfranchised Black Americans. W.D. Mohammed articulates this in the following passages:

> He (Fard Muhammad) told the Hon. E. Muhammad we were a baby nation but that is not an insult because we were in the beginning organization in its infancy and he called us the baby Nation of Islam. If what he established was a baby Nation of Islam then what would that baby nation be when it grows up and becomes a nation of men? It would be just what you are looking at under Imam W. Deen Muhammad. So it was a powerful psychology with that power unless they know the wisdom of scripture.[7]

Furthermore, in another passage he states the following:

> Fard Muhammad planned to bring the Nation of Islam to the purity of Al-Islam. . . . We repeat the verse, "Destroy this temple and I will rebuild it in three days." I said earlier that Mr. Fard saw how to perform his role and that G-d blessed him to see how they did their thing. So he said I come in dyed garments and I'm sure that he planned his thing to self destroy. So his saying also without verbalizing it "Destroy this Temple," and didn't he call it temple? He called his house temple not Mosque, the holy temple of Islam.[8]

Starting at a young age, W.D. Mohammed was trained via private tutors. At elementary and high school levels, he studied at the University of Islam, a private school system established by Clara Muhammad, the wife of Elijah Muhammad in the 1930s throughout the United States that educated Muslim boys and girls from grades four through twelve and offered general school subjects, Islamic education, and the Arabic language. During the early days of the school's existence, the Detroit Board of Education, through which it began its operations, sought to close it down and return the students to public schools. As the early Nation of Islam worked to establish its community, several Muslim teachers, including Elijah Muhammad, were arrested for what was labeled as contributing to the delinquency of minors per instructions given to Elijah Muhammad by WD Fard. At the University of Islam, W.D. Mohammed was taught by senior members of the community who were affectionately called "Pioneers" as a term of endearment and respect. They included Sheikh James Shabazz, Brother Louis X, Lester X, Farraz Jordan, and Sisters Lois X, Suzie X, and Susan X Douglas, to name a few. In addition, W.D. Mohammed privately studied the Qur'an as a religious text, in a manner similar to that of young children throughout the broader Muslim world, and was privately taught Arabic grammar, morphology, syntax, logic, and recitation from various native Arabic speakers mainly from the Middle East, including Professor Jamil Diab, an Arab of Palestinian heritage, and Muhammad Abdullah.[9]

W.D. Mohammed was the seventh son of his father and was raised closely in the strong religious and hierarchal control of the Nation of Islam. Even Fard Muhammad and Elijah Muhammad made W.D. Mohammed's unique role part of the community's popular lore. W.D. Mohammed captures this in the following statement:

> The power of mystery. The other children were already born when Fard Muhammad came. I was the only child born during his stay with us. I was chosen because a new baby, new birth—they wanted a Christ figure, someone with a mystery about [him]. Here was this newborn baby predicted by Fard Muhammad to be a male and it so happened the guess was right. I say a "guess" not to laugh at our religion. I say "guess" because that's the language the honorable Elijah Muhammad used.[10]

However, for over fourteen years, W.D. Mohammed repeatedly engaged in ideological conflicts with his father and was excommunicated at least four times over differences of opinion based on his nonorthodox tenets with normative Islam and his refusal to accept the God image given to his father by Fard Muhammad. During this time, W.D. Mohammed used the Qur'an, without the religious commentary of his father or Fard, as his source of inspiration and divine guidance.[11] When he was suspended from the Nation of Islam in 1965, he was not reinstated until 1969.

During this time he ran a bookstore and formed a study group called the Upliftment Society. He also worked as a welder and ran other small businesses, including a carpet and furniture cleaning service. When he was finally reinstated, he did not regain his title as a minister until 1974, one year before the death of his father.

Entering into the 1970s, the Nation of Islam suffered serious setbacks including the loss of members after the assassination of Malcolm X, internal conflicts in the Muhammad family, and Elijah Muhammad's ongoing health challenges. By the late 1970s, the Nation of Islam had built an empire valued at more than $85,000,000. It had acquired more than 15,000 acres of farmland in states throughout the United States; a thriving newspaper called *Muhammad Speaks*; tractor trailers; banks; an airplane; and numerous other mosques and properties in America and abroad, including in the Caribbean, Africa, and Europe.

When W.D. Mohammed was reinstated back into the organization in 1974, he was given responsibility at the mosque in Chicago. During this time, his rhetoric was extremely provocative, including statements and religious dogma that openly opposed his father's teachings that were rooted in black nationalism and proto-Islamic concepts. During this same year, Elijah Muhammad was repeatedly informed of W.D. Mohammed's open critique against the Nation of Islam's rhetoric and dogma, and on one instance Elijah Muhammad summoned his son to listen with him to one of his sermons in which Elijah informs him, "my son's got it, my son can go anywhere on earth and preach."[12] He later began the process of transferring power to W.D. Mohammed. Elijah Muhammad would die on January 29 of the next year of congestive heart failure; and on February 26, 1975, at the annual Saviors Day convention, an annual celebration in which the communities of the Nation of Islam came together, Abass Rassoull, the National Secretary of the Nation of Islam, announced that W.D. Mohammed had been chosen to lead the Nation of Islam. The announcement of W.D. Mohammed shocked the crowd as he had kept a low profile up to that point. Nevertheless, W.D. Mohammed had been considered the chosen child and predicted by Fard Muhammad to be the successor to Elijah.

Despite their long-term disagreement, W.D. Mohammed was able, upon his father's death, to institute new reforms and reorganize, dismantle, and decentralize the strong command that the Nation of Islam had maintained throughout the United States. He immediately instituted these changes by first renaming the organization from the Nation of Islam to the World Community of Al-Islam in the West (WCIW). By shifting the name and moving the community away from the old Nation of Islam belief systems, W.D. Mohammed was ushering the community into the Qur'anic teachings as practiced by the Muslim community throughout the world. According to Dr.

Sulayman Nyang, retired professor of Howard University and an authority on Islam in America, W.D. Mohammed's efforts were twofold:

> One [was] the re-Islamization of the movement; the second, the re-Americanization of the movement. Here's a man who inherited an organization that most scholars of Islam would describe as heretical before [Mohammed took over].... That mythology has been replaced by sound theology rooted in Islamic orthodoxy. The people had to make a 180-degree turn.[13]

COMMUNITY AND PHILOSOPHICAL MIND-SET

Through this purposeful effort, W.D. Mohammed rebranded the social-cultural movement of the Nation of Islam as an orthodox Muslim community in a way that allowed it to gain acceptance in America and legitimacy in the broader Muslim world as a whole. As part of this rebranding, he instituted a number of changes that shifted the original structure of the Nation of Islam. At the core of his efforts was the dismantling of the racial superiority doctrine of Elijah Muhammad, followed by sweeping reforms to radically differentiate his teachings from those of his father. He created a new frame for the entire movement that included the following changes: (1) labeling Fard Muhammad, the founder of the Nation, as a wise man instead of "God in person" as Elijah Muhammad and followers had considered him; (2) restoring and honoring Malcolm X's legacy as a critical and influential member in the movement and raising his status to that of an important contributor to the Nation of Islam as an organization; (3) raising the status of American citizenship as a central role in the new rebranded movement, a direct critique on the Nation of Islam's previous rhetoric calling for a separate state; and (4) doctrinally ensuring that the followers of the previous Nation of Islam were in line with traditional and normative Islam through ritual devotional acts as commonly practiced by Muslims throughout the world. Finally, but most important, W.D. Mohammed used the Qur'an itself and the words of G-d to guide his efforts to radically change his community, including the following verse from the Qur'an as part of his religious framing: "He who created me, will also guide me."[14]

W.D. Mohammed used this verse repeatedly to support his argument that G-d guided and directly intervened in the affairs of his community, largely without the support and assistance of foreign influences, including his co-religionists throughout the broader Arab and Islamic world. W.D. Mohammed would also argue that his theological framing and support built on other great Black American pioneers, including Harriet Tubman, who often referred to "consulting God" in her affairs as she led her people out of bondage in the American South.[15]

The institution of these new measures provided W.D. Mohammed with the foundational basis to establish a new movement on the theological and spiritual grounds of the religion of Islam. Through weekly radio addresses, public events using audio and cassette recordings, and annual conventions, he used his new platform to directly critique the theological misgivings of his father. Under the leadership of Elijah Muhammad, the movement believed that African Americans were Asiatic descendants of the tribe of Shabazz. This concept introduced by Elijah Muhammad likely came about as part of a re-imagination by both Elijah Muhammad and Fard Muhammad to create a narrative of Islamic and African history for the upliftment of African Americans. W.D. Mohammed made sure to confront head-on these previously held beliefs as outlined by Elijah Muhammad. He highlighted legitimate and historically factual events in African and Islamic history not only to connect his followers to a past using empirical research and data but also to connect the African American population as a whole to a history of African Islamic heritage.[16]

For this purpose, W.D. Mohammed introduced the term "Bilalians." Bilal was an Ethiopian Muslim who was born in 600 AD. His role in early Islamic history is of primary importance as he was one of the first converts to Islam, and he was brutally punished by his slave master in the pre-Islamic/Arabian society for his refusal to denounce Islam. According to authoritative Islamic accounts, Bilal would lament and cry out his belief in monotheism and his faith in the new religion of Islam as the early Muslim community was emerging. By moving the community away from the previous narrative of Asiatics and, instead, recentering Islamic identity and blackness to the religion of Islam overall and to the continent of Africa overall, W.D. Mohammed created a sense of belonging and meaning by creating a new imagery that allowed the followers of the Nation of Islam to have a hero and model who was both black and Muslim. The *Muhammad Speaks* newspaper, the publication of the Nation of Islam, was renamed the *Bilalian News*, effective November 1, 1975, furthering the change carried out by W.D. Mohammed. The introduction of Bilal during this time was an experiment by W.D. Mohammed and his followers in creating a stronger foothold of orthodoxy and legitimacy within mainstream Muslim circles. Even W.D. Mohammed was keen on the delicate balance between being seen as appropriating Bilal for his community's purpose and possibly being seen as having left the extreme ethnocentric identity of the Nation of Islam for another idea of racial superiority within Sunni orthodoxy. W.D. Mohammed said, "We are experimenting . . . trying to find a solution to our identity problem." "But," he goes on to say, "Bilalian didn't work for us. We were charged with a division in Islam, of making Bilal our leader rather than the Prophet."[17] In the *Bilalian News* on November 16, 1979, he defended the slow reform toward Sunni Islam that he was trying to introduce to members of the former Nation of Islam. In regards to the concept of Bilalian, he states that it

> is not a religious name. We have adopted the name Bilalian as an ethnic name to replace other terms that we think are not as rich, ethnically speaking. They are not as rich because to identify with skin color is not as rich ethnically speaking as to identify with an ancestor who identified with a great ideology.... We don't identify with Bilal only because he was Muslim, it's mainly because he was an African ancestor.[18]

In 1975, while widespread reforms were taking place outwardly in regards to organization, spiritual and religious aspects of the movement were also undergoing radical change. W.D. Mohammed changed the rituals and dress code of the membership as well as the internal aesthetics of the buildings. Previously, the religious houses of the old Nation of Islam were called mosques or temples, which oftentimes was a misnomer because they did not host Islamic devotional prayers as performed in the greater Islamic world. More often than not, Fard Muhammad and Elijah Muhammad used these terms to introduce the community to certain Islamic concepts, but they were limited in their ability to provide fully normative understanding of this terminology to the masses. Equally important, a "mosque" became a "Masjid," the Arabic term for an Islamic house of worship. Gone were the slogans that used anti-American or Anti-Christian rhetoric; now there was a slow introduction of Arabic religious symbols, words, and grammar into the private and public lexicon. Furthermore, seats were removed from the numerous Nation of Islam buildings across America, replaced by carpets, and the five daily prayers led by an imam trained by W.D. Mohammed and his associates were starting to take place. During this year and the years to come, as the religious beliefs, rituals, and practices of the emergent new Muslim community began to take form, W.D. Mohammed began to break down the strict dress code and grooming requirements of the Nation of Islam. Gone were the days of the required bow tie and suits for men and the matching tunic style clothing for women who were part of the movement. Instead, W.D. Mohammed encouraged his followers to wear clothing that was modest and clean and that did not degrade their religion by being the only requirement.[19]

In 1976, the year after W.D. Mohammed took over as leader of the new Nation of Islam, he formally established the WCIW. Seeking to differentiate himself from the Nation of Islam of his father, he utilized this new name to best characterize his community's experience of being Muslims in America and, at the same time, to differentiate the community from the ideology and teachings of the former Nation of Islam. The change of doctrine also brought about considerable resistance from and challenges by certain segments of the organization who resisted these massive overhauls. The most significant defection from the organization was that of the international spokesperson,

Louis Farrakhan, who announced his departure in December 1977. Farrakhan disagreed with W.D. Mohammed's approach and decided to reject his teachings and continue to follow the doctrine of the old Nation of Islam. Farrakhan believed that the move to orthodox Islam was a rejection of Elijah Muhammad and that the sweeping changes, including increased autonomy of individual mosques, created a lack of discipline in the movement. Thus, Farrakhan rebranded himself as the national representative of Elijah Muhammad and created *Final Call*, a new weekly publication that featured Elijah Muhammad on the front cover and brought back the beliefs and core values of the original Nation of Islam to continue its efforts.

Even today Farrakhan still carries forward the mantle of the Nation of Islam and its beliefs, but in 2012 he appointed Imam Sultan Muhammad, the great-grandson of Elijah Muhammad, as resident imam of the Nation of Islam to Mosque Maryam, the flagship mosque in Chicago. Imam Sultan Muhammad presides over Islamic prayers; birth, funereal, and other ceremonial functions; and Arabic language instruction to the community, thus suggesting that the struggle to uphold the old belief system of the Nation against the shift and pressure of religious orthodoxy continues today.[20]

INTELLECTUAL TEACHING
AND LANGUAGE OF IMAM W.D. MOHAMMED

From the period of 1975 to 2008, W.D. Mohammed traveled across America and the world promoting interfaith cooperation and establishing a legacy to provide the groundwork for his intellectual and theological movement. By establishing normative Islamic practices in mainstream American society, he created the foundation for other Muslim communities. Seeking to gain respect of his coreligionists, W.D. Mohammed globetrotted throughout the world to gain the audience of anyone willing to listen to his reformist ideas and embrace the concept of global Islam. One such event was the First Islamic Conference of North America sponsored by the Muslim World League in April 1977. W.D. Mohammed spoke at this event, which brought together delegates from 169 Muslim organizations, centers, mosques, institutions, and societies from across the United States and Canada. Its sole aim was to bring the global Muslim world together with Muslims in North America in order to help them understand each other's challenges and acknowledge the diversity of Muslims throughout the world. On this occasion, W.D. Mohammed was introduced as the chief imam of the WCIW and provided the following statements:

> Distinguished delegates! Assalamu Alaikum wa Rahmatullah. I would like to first speak of some pluses for us in America. There have been many minuses, but we have realized over the last two years so many pluses that I don't think

we should worry about those minuses anymore. Two years ago, through the Honorable Elijah Muhammad, the late leader of the Nation of Islam in America, may he rest in peace, Allah blessed this community and through this man wanted to make a change and he made the change. He said to his people on his sick bed while death was on him that Islam is not a race. Islam is a nation. And he said to his officers, "I am with my son Wallace D. Muhammad. I am with him so that he can go and preach the religion of Islam everywhere in our community." That was a big change. The same father that had prevented his son from expressing pure Islamic teachings to his followers made the change and said that the son can go and preach freely in our community. From that day on we have been making progress and I can tell you today there is no preaching of any foreign or contrary ideas in our community called the World Community of Islam in the West. We were taught at one time that the black man is the God and we were given black supremacy so that it would give us a sense of superiority and dignity in a world that had held us down under white supremacy, and we were taught that the devil is the creation of God and when I assumed leadership I told our community that the devil is not the creation of God. God created the jinn and he did not create the jinn to be the devil. . . .

We plan for the first time to lead a delegation of 300 Muslims. I hope we have people who have committed themselves and we hope to have 300 Muslims making the hajj this year, inshallah. That will be a big thing to see 300 Bilalian Americans, 300 Afro American Muslims going together with all the Muslims of the world in the spirit of true brotherhood to make hajj. So we hope for this, and pray for us and pray for our success. . . . And lastly, I want to say that I am not a new convert to the Sunnah of the Prophet Muhammad. It was in 1967 that I made hajj and when I made that hajj I made a pledge to myself and Allah. I said that from this day on I will not tolerate any deviations, I will not support any religious deviations, I will not tolerate any religious deviations from others especially from my family. From that day on I have been fighting openly, and I thank Allah for blessing me to live and encouraging me and giving me the blessing of America and inside of America, blessing me with strong support from the World Community of Islam.[21]

In 1977, W.D. Mohammed was responsible for leading this delegation on hajj as articulated to the Muslim World League. This was the largest delegation of indigenous American Muslims in history to travel to the holy precincts in Saudi Arabia. In 1978, as part of his many efforts to reform the Nation of Islam's teachings, he established the Committee to Remove All Racial Images of the Divine (CRAID). This movement energized significant dialogue among Christians and Muslims around the issue of racial images in worship. This dialogue included African American churches throughout America that, despite having a congregation that was largely or exclusively African American, were displaying pictures of a white Jesus, and the early WCIW community was vocal in its critique of this practice.[22]

In the 1980s and 1990s, W.D. Mohammed built some of his strongest and most meaningful relationships with the broader Muslim world. During this period of time, he worked hard to balance his relationships with various

Muslim communities in the broader Islamic world to include Africans, Arabs, Southeast Asians, and other Muslims of various ideological traditions as a show of pan-Islamic solidarity, but he also seemed to be aware of the attachment that came with these new relationships. Like his father, he formed close ties to the former Egyptian president Gamal Abdul Nasser and maintained a cordial relationship with Anwar El Sadat. In 1957, Elijah Muhammad sent the following letter to Abdel Nasser in honor of the Afro-Asian Solidarity Conference:

> Lt. President G.A. Nasser
> In the Name of Allah, the Beneficent, the Merciful, Beloved Brothers of Africa and Asia:
>
> As-Salaamu Alaikum. Your long lost Muslim Brothers here in America pray that Allah's Divine presence will be felt at this historical African-Asian Conference, and give unity to our efforts for peace and brotherhood. Freedom, Justice and Equality for all Africans and Asians is of far reaching importance, not only to you of the East but also to over seventeen million of your long lost brothers of African and Asian descent here in the West. May Allah open and guide the hearts and minds of our people who are acting as our rulers and our leaders and especially those who are participating in this great Conference. . . .
>
> All Success is with Allah As-Salaam-Alaikum
> Your long-lost brothers of the West
> Elijah Muhammad[23]

Two years later, President Abdel Nasser reciprocated Elijah Muhammad's message of unity and goodwill. James R. Lawson, president of the United African Nationalists Movement, delivered a message on his behalf at the Nation of the Islam's 1959 annual convention:

> I would like to convey my words to our brother peoples; namely, that unity and solidarity are the two most indispensable factors for realizing our liberty. This lesson must be seriously taken to heart and maintained against imperialist forces seeking to undermine our integrity and convert us into disintegrated groups which can easily be victimized and made to serve their selfish interests. . . . Our great religion and traditions and ways of living will serve as the cornerstone in building the new society based on right, justice and equality.[24]

Even the late Dr. Akbar Muhammad, W.D. Mohammed's brother, was a beneficiary of the close relationship between the Nation of Islam and the Egyptian government and received a scholarship to study at the prestigious Al-Azhar University, the beacon of Sunni Islamic scholarship, and became a fluent Arabic speaker.[25] C. Eric Lincoln noted that W.D. Mohammed was the only American observer invited to attend the Tenth Annual Islamic Conference of Ministers of Foreign Affairs in Fez, Morocco.[26] In this same time period, the Arab Gulf States appointed W.D. Mohammed as the official consultant and trustee to lead proselytization activities in America for the distribution of missionary funds. He was also given the responsibility of certifying Americans who applied for Saudi visas in order to make the hajj to Mecca, perhaps suggesting that Gulf Arab states were recognizing the importance of the Black American emergent Sunni Muslim community and the role W.D. Mohammed would play. Furthermore, during the first Gulf War in the early 1990s, W.D. Mohammed was quite supportive of the coalition efforts between America and its Gulf Arab partners. However, by 1994, W.D. Mohammed seemed to have recognized the cost associated with having a close relationship with Saudi Arabia, the custodian of the two holy precincts. In an interview with the *Los Angeles Times* in 1999, W.D. Mohammed asserts:

> I don't receive any money now, but I have received some and I lost it . . . because I suspected some strings were attached. I said I can't accept this kind of relationship. They were choosing my friends for me, too. The enemy of the friends who were giving me money was supposed to by my enemy, too.[27]

Despite the low-visibility, institution-building framework he had built up for his community in America from the 1970s to the 1990s, from the mid-1990s onward, W.D. Mohammed was forced to make some major changes that likely inspired him to embark on a mission to create a language of interpretation for the American Muslim perspective.

REFORMATION

After inheriting and radically transforming the community of his father, W.D. Mohammed underwent a religious binary, one living under the shadow of his father's old legacy and the other his tenuous relationship between immigrant and overseas Muslims. I would argue that he used the period from the mid-1990s until his death in 2008 to firmly root his community in the American experience while preserving his Islamic heritage and, ultimately, his Black American Islamic heritage on his own terms. Building on the tradition of his previously mentioned ancestral African Islamic reformers like Al Hajj Salim Suwari, Usman Dan Fodio, Ibrahim Niasse, and Amadou Bamba Mbacke, he was able to get his community to move beyond a historical African Islamic identity and embrace a broader Islamic reformation movement. His reformative work transcended locations and involved similar religious motifs such as individuals from the late nineteenth and early twentieth centuries such as Jamal al-Din Afghani and Muhammad Abduh of Egypt or Abdolkarim Soroush of Iran. Furthermore, I argue that W.D. Mohammed community reform is not to be seen simply as Black American Muslims seeking to regurgitate the liturgical and religious tradition of old world Sunni Islam as argued by Jackson and a desired end state of being replicas of their religious brethren globally: instead, my argument of Black American Muslims as invoked by W.D. Mohammed, is one rooted in a tradition based in new language, identity, and experience while using the Qur'an itself as its foundation rather than perceived binding religious frameworks of centuries past.

The approach of W.D. Mohammed and his community does not always coincide with those of other historically Black American Sunni Muslims; in fact, there have been some serious disagreements. Many Black American Sunni Muslims—such as the community of Imam Jamil Abdullah Al-Amin, the former civil rights firebrand and Black Panther known as H Rap Brown, and individuals like Imam Zaid Shakir, the eulogist of Muhammad Ali and the cofounder and presiding imam of Zaytuna College, the first Muslim liberal arts college in America—argue that the religious practices of W.D. Mohammed and his adherents were not well-grounded in knowledge of centuries-old traditional Sunni Islamic texts and commentaries. Ihsan Bagby, a professor of Islamic studies at the University of Kentucky, who is himself Muslim and African American, captures this critical issue in the following assessment:

> African American Muslims come to Islam carrying African American and American cultural experiences (foremost the Black Church and the street), and the questions arise: How much of that unique African American culture is to be left behind? . . . To what extent should African American Muslims follow the traditional practices of the Muslim world, which is the culture that immigrant Muslims bear?[28]

A similar, yet different critique of W.D. Mohammed was also given by immigrant and overseas Muslims. Besides the obvious differences in language, the cultural and class disparities and differences in religious interpretation also caused serious challenges as the communities interacted. Mosques affiliated with W.D. Mohammed seemed to lack the formality and use of ceremonial rituals that many immigrant and overseas Muslims were accustomed to experiencing when visiting an Islamic place of worship. The often choppy and inconsistent use of Arabic in formal prayer, the casual nature of prayer service, and the call and response exchange, similar to the African American church experience, have led many to be highly critical of W.D. Mohammed's Islamic pedagogical approach and bonafides.[29] Sherman Jackson—a noted Islamic scholar, professor at the University of Southern California, and the author of *Islam and the Blackamerican*—argues that Muslims, whether they are Black American or immigrants, find themselves in a conundrum with W.D. Mohammed. In the immediate aftermath of his death in

2008, Jackson penned an article to the broader Black American Muslim community in which he critiqued how W.D. Mohammed's reformation activities were perceived by Black American Sunnis at large and how his followers' inability to master basic Arabic and Islamic sciences was viewed as making them in some way unauthentic Muslims.[30]

W.D. Mohammed was not immune to the external critique and internally sought to address it by urging his imams to become better grounded in Islam and Arabic and by forging relationships globally, including sending younger students in his association overseas. His aim was to encourage his students to rethink Islam and establish their own independent Islamic thinking, all of this while they were interacting with other Muslim communities including in Malaysia and Syria. In 2000, he established a formal partnership to enroll students from his association to study at the prestigious Abu Nour Islamic Institute in Damascus, Syria. Founded in the 1930s, the Abu Nour community aimed to promote Islamic religious sciences as well as spiritual practices and missionary activities that foster interfaith dialogue worldwide.[31] The young Muslims who were emissaries of the W.D. Mohammed community were sent there to enhance their knowledge and then return to their respective communities so as to aid members in Islamic and Arabic sciences—Qur'anic recitation, memorization, grammar, morphology, and so on—but most important, to be of benefit to Islam in America. During this time overseas, the students were confronted with the challenge of how to reconcile their American and Muslim identities, constantly processing and thinking of their role and purpose as they were learning new sacred knowledge. During the students' time overseas, W.D. Mohammed, in his weekly news publication, provided commentary from some of the letters he received from the students as well as larger social commentary regarding issues with which the American Muslim community was confronted.[32] In the *Muslim Journal* in 2005, W.D. Mohammed remarked,

> In Islam we have our own mannerisms. We shouldn't take our mannerisms from the schools of thought that were established before the discovery of America. . . . As scholars and students we can benefit from studying those schools of thought about different situations which will help us. But as leaders, we should be defining what is proper behavior and manners in the home, in the public places and in the workplace. So there is a lot of work for us.[33]

Despite the critique of his Islamic methodological approach from his co-religionists, W.D. Mohammed's efforts toward Islamic reform had been a part of his aim and objective ever since the days of his departure from his father's movement. His interpretation of Islam rooted in the American context is similar to the Islamic revivalist movements of the medieval and early Islamic periods. Particularly, he offered a nonlegalistic approach toward interpreting Islamic scripture through a values-based view of Islam that was unattached to the cultural norms and filters of the broader Islamic world. His approach toward Islam was a constructive theological one, in which he offered new, fresh views of the faith that allowed contemporary Muslims to relate to their past while profoundly living in the present. He built on other academic bodies of work, including that of Yehuda Kurtzer, a scholar of contemporary Jewish history, who discusses similar themes such as how to reconcile memory of the Jewish past while forging forward in the present.[34] While addressing issues such as race, extremism, and interfaith dialogue, W.D. Mohammed promoted American values balanced with faith, a view that, at the time, was seen by many in the mainstream Muslim community as heretical. In the contemporary context, however, and in the era of the so-called Islamic State and al-Qa'ida, his perspective seems rather timely.

Having made efforts to encourage patriotism in his community by creating an internal American patriotism day and making sure the American flag appeared on the front page of his newspaper and the national anthem was invoked at public and private events (including at mosques), W.D. Mohammed can now be viewed as a strident defender of America.[35] W.D. Mohammed's textual, spiritual, and nonliteralist interpretation of the Qur'an was consistent with the approaches of other revivalist Muslims who sought to preserve and reinterpret Islamic traditions in light of historical and contemporary conditions. Using the English language as an ally, he purposefully ushered in a new lexicon that at times seemed at odds with Muslim puritans. He sought a strategy for bring about changes to a stale and outdated hermeneutic tradition that, in his view, needed to be filtered through his own Black American Muslim experience. W.D. Mohammed is not alone in this undertaking. American Islamic scholar Muqtedar Khan argues that the Islamic faith suffers from narrow legalistic interpretation:

> The Islamic intellectual tradition—which includes Islamic legal thought (*Usul al fiqh* and fiqh) theology (*kalam*), mysticism (tasawwuf) and philosophy (*falsafa*)— is one of the most developed and profound traditions of human knowledge. In the area of political philosophy, however, this intellectual heritage remains strikingly underdeveloped. One of the reasons for this lacuna is the "colonial" tendency of Islamic legal thought. Many Islamic jurists simply equate Islam with Islamic law (Shariah) and privilege the study of the latter. As a result we have only episodic exploration of the idea of a polity in Islam. Hundreds of Islamic schools and universities now produce hundreds of thousands of Islamic legal scholars but hardly any produce political theorists or philosophers. With some rare exceptions, this intellectual poverty has reduced Islamic thought to the status of a medieval legal tradition.[36]

In *The Sublime Qur'an*, Laleh Bakhtiar offers a feminist reading of the Qur'an, keeping the spiritual essence of the Qur'anic injunctions while providing fresh insights that are relevant and time specific to the Western and

American Muslim audience. Shadaab Rahemutulla, in *Qur'an of the Oppressed*, offers yet another compelling reinterpretation that helps modern Muslims perceive an array of social challenges ranging from race, poverty, interfaith issues, and gender imbalances in Muslim and non-Muslim nations. I would argue that it was the work of W.D. Mohammed, who had the courage to confront societal taboos at a time when it was more difficult to do so, created the conditions for individuals like Bakhtiar and Rahemutulla, as well as groups and movements to feel comfortable publicly challenging mainstream Muslim and non-Muslim audiences without feeling persecution.[37] By offering Martin Luther–type reforms in the American Muslim community, W.D. Mohammed sought to create an Islamic narrative filtered through the Black American experience on his own terms. By using particularist language suitable for his constituents who were second-, third-, and fourth-generation Black American Muslim converts, he was seeking to bring about a gradual change while being sensitive to Black American life. For example, the introduction of word choices, such as the use of "Al-Islam"—the definitive form of the Arabic word *Islam*—to demarcate his community's desire to get back to the original teachings of Islam in its simplistic form without all the cultural baggage, was essential to W.D. Mohammed's language and message. He also used simplified English terms instead of Arabic when describing the *Sunna* or way of Muhammad, using instead "the life example of Muhammad" so as to demonstrate the emphasis on lifestyle and a code of conduct based on how Prophet Muhammad lived rather than emphasizing empty Arabic phrases that his adherents couldn't connect with.

Furthermore, his use of "G-d," placing a hyphen between the letters to describe God, the divine, omnipotent, and all-powerful creator, was a purposeful attempt to more broadly define his community's commentary on Islamic theological matters and religious interpretation, and it also showed that he stood in solidarity with his Jewish counterparts who sought to avoid writing a name of the creator or defacing the name.[38] Also evident in W.D. Mohammed's speech, public lectures, and writings is a plain and simple approach to religion as a whole and the Qur'an in particular. He saw the Qur'an as a practical book that spoke to the common man and that could be articulated and explained through the experiences of everyday life. In his Qur'anic translations and exegesis, he expressed these ideas in the overall vocabulary and how he related to his religious text in simple English. This is evident, in one of W.D. Mohammed's Arabic to English translations, of the opening chapter of the Qur'an. He states,

> With G-d's name, the merciful benefactor, the merciful redeemer. All Praises are due to G-d, the Guardian Evolver, The Cherisher and Sustainer of All Systems of Knowledge. The Merciful Benefactor, the Merciful Redeemer. The Sole Judge on the day of religion. We worship you only and we turn to you

begging for assistance. Guide us on the straight path, the way of those on whom you bestow blessings not those who incur wrath nor those who go astray.[39]

W.D. Mohammed also argued that his followers should confront and engage the Qur'an and the life example of Muhammad's history themselves. He felt that they should not rely on others to interpret for them but instead should offer solutions themselves. In a speech in Harlem, New York, he provided a roadmap for his community and offered the clearest evidence of establishing an American Islamic narrative free from the cultural and intra-Muslim pitfalls affecting the broader Muslim world. "They say, 'Well, what do you have here, Brother Imam, that makes you so special?'" the Imam asked rhetorically. "'The Qur'an, the Word of God,' he said. 'You mean to tell me that just you, and the Word of God . . . ?' 'That's right, just me and the Word of God.'" For W.D. Mohammed, independent interpretation was essential, and it required that his followers relied less on non-Black Muslim brothers and sisters. "It is not enough for God to tell us through another race; we still feel insecure," W.D. Mohammed said. "We feel unapproved that we still have not been validated by man. They are the master, and we are the boys."[40] And, to amplify this point, he frequently used the following two Qur'anic passages to establish his authoritative bonafides using the Qur'an alone as the blueprint for his intellectual and spiritual mission, "He is the one who has created me and is the one who guides me" and "Only the one who created me; and indeed, He will guide me"[41] to validate his arguments.

To maintain and strengthen this independence, W.D. Mohammed appointed Imam Darnell Karim of Chicago, his childhood friend and a leading imam and Qur'anic reciter in the community, and Imam Vernon Fareed of Norfolk, Virginia, to carry out a project of translating and reciting the Qur'an. The translation would use W.D. Mohammed's commentary, or *tafsir*, and the recitation would be performed by Darnell Karim, who was trained by native Arabic speakers alongside W.D. Mohammed as a child.[42]

W.D. Mohammed also provided religious and social commentary on numerous points.

On why he did not follow a *Madhab* or formal School of Thought:

> It's because, as I understand, the *madhabs* are geographically influenced. We are in a totally different geography in America. And I don't think we should adhere to any madhabs because those were influenced by their location and they are different based on their location. The Shafi school and the Maliki school in North Africa and the Wahhabi one in Saudi Arabia. Regions are supposed to develop these madhabs. I think we are gradually getting a sense of *madhabs* in America, especially those like me. We are getting a sense of *madhabs*. And with the coming generation I think that we will be getting a much stronger sense of it. It is coming more and more.[43]

On African American independent thinking:

> We must establish our intellect and the way to do it is to think for the betterment of our people and not look to others (outside of the African American) for answers. We must establish our own independent thinking! Independent thinking that benefits and solves problems for us and benefits us, solves problems and improves the state of our people on this earth, firstly in this country America and (secondly) on this earth (the African diaspora). As a Muslim I devote my mind to that. I have never stopped devoting my mind to that. As far as I can go back in my life my mind has been devoted to that as a Muslim, also as an African American and I'm going to be more vocal and call the attention of you (who are under my leadership) and our African American people to that need to establish an intelligentsia for the African American people. [44]

On how we are to establish Muslim life in America:

> We need to extend our forces by recognizing other powerful allies that may not be Muslims but share our basic sense of values and are aspiring for the same healthy life of the human being. At the same time realize also that there is a situation of incompatibility and a situation of compatibility.
>
> We have Al-Islam in our lives, and it makes us different. Some of you are not aware of that. To not be aware of this is to put yourself in a bad situation. Al-Islam should be seen as your distinction. If you are not different, then something is terribly wrong. An African American Muslim is not to be just typical of African Americans. An African American Muslim should be distinguished among the African American crowds. To try to distinguish yourself by wearing a fez or the Nehru suit or Pakistani dress or the cloaks of the Saudis is not enough. That will not help you reach the goal line of the "black" race. For anyone can go to Hollywood or to the TV sets and see actors wearing such dress. I wear American dress. However, I also see my brothers who are African American and are wearing eastern clothes, and I do not disrespect them. I see them and hope they do have the distinct Islamic life and are just covered in those clothes. I am hoping that they do have the substance of the Islamic life. But when I see one that is just under covers without that religious substance, it hurts. [45]

On Muslims being in the military:

> When you join the military make sure you have the mind for it, your spirit is with it, if not don't join. So far it's still a voluntary army. They are talking about drafting but that hasn't come yet. So you don't have to be in the military if you don't want to, if your spirit is not with it, if your mind is not with it, it helps all of us by not joining the military. But if you have your spirit with it and you feel as I do that this is a sacred duty and that we have a life of great value here that we shouldn't ask others to go and defend and we not be willing to defend it, then please join the military and be a great soldier for the United States of America and for all good Americans. [46]

On jihad:

> We think Jihad in Al Islam that it means struggle, Jihad has also been published as holy war in Al Islam; it is a holy war to hold on to my good nature when I'm tempted to do wrong on every side and everywhere I look there is temptation all around, this is holy war. The fight to keep my good nature that is the holy war, that is the holiest of wars.[47]

On the Qur'an to be read in context:

> You can't just read what is in the Quran and deal with it as though it is nothing but words. No. Those words have a social, spiritual context, a political context. They have a context. They fit in a particular focus, a particular framework, and they also have a short time context, a time framework, etc. That is not all there is to it.[48]

On Western democracy and freedom:

> Here is the difference between what Islam wants for society and what America wants for society. In principle, America and Islam want the same thing for man. That's in principle. But in practice, they are different. America seems to put the emphasis and light on freedom, more so than on justice. The result is that the society is turned on to freedom, but not necessarily turned on to justice. My freedom, then, will disrespect your freedom, and my freedom may clash with your freedom. Then the society suffers, because we are going after freedom, but have lost the connection of freedom with justice. Freedom and justice are born together and are to live together always. You can never separate justice from freedom.[49]

W.D. Mohammed represents revivalism organically rooted in the American experience. Through his emphasis on a values-based approach toward understanding his faith, he was able to both make Islam accessible to the American and, through his students, gain acceptance and recognition of his efforts in the Muslim mainstream.[50] Through his tireless efforts to normalize Islam in the American public lexicon and by creating a legacy that paved the way for two Muslim congressmen, as well as countless doctors, lawyers, and ordinary Americans, W.D. Mohammed posthumously became, in a sense, the patron saint of American Islam, the *Shaykul Islam* or the highest Islamic religious leader, thus fulfilling the prediction made on the day of his birth. In many ways, his spiritual, religious, and intellectual teachings carried in the tradition of other American Muslim revivalists, including Fazlur Rahman (1919–1988), who was a Pakistani American scholar known globally as a leading architect of modernist Qur'anic exegesis.[51] In closing, Imam W.D. Mohammed will be immortalized in his grave more than when he was alive. He created a cultural, theological, and religious narrative that fused a unique American style.

Before formal institutions established to represent Muslims in the United States, such as Muslim Student Association (MSA), Islamic Society of North America (ISNA), Zaytuna, and others, were flourishing, the men and women who broke away from the liturgical tradition of the Nation of Islam made a radical shift to open doors in small towns throughout the country in order to make inroads toward coexistence in America. Only time will show the long-term impact of W.D. Mohammed's influence in America and his contributions to immigrant and overseas Muslims, but his strategy and legacy provided a cognitive opening for Islam to make its way into mainstream America through the son of a former black nationalist leader. This, in turn, provides positive lessons in directing individuals to channel their real and/or perceived grievances in a way that allows them to become fully integrated, contributing members of American society, thus suggesting the possibility of global opportunities in the era of transnational terrorism and violence.

NOTES

1. From his time coming into office as the leader in 1975, Wallace Muhammad used many different spellings for his name, including the Arabic name of "Warithudeen."
2. Zafar Ishaq Ansari, "WD Muhammad: The Making of a 'Black Muslim' Leader (1933–1961)," *American Journal of Islamic Social Sciences* 2, no. 2 (1985): 248–62. W. Deen Muhammad, *Focus on Al-Islam: A Series of Interveiews with Imam W. Deen Muhammad in Pittsburgh, Pennslyvania* (Chicago: Zakat Publications, 1988), 35–37.
3. Warith Deen Muhammad, *Al-Islam: Unity & Leadership* (Chicago: Sense Maker, 1991), 102–3.
4. Elijah Muhammad, *Message to the Blackman in America*, (n.p.:United Brothers Communication Systems, 196).
5. Clifton E. Marsh, *From Black Muslims to Muslims: The Transition from Seperatism to Islam, 1930–1980* (Metuchen, NJ: Scarecrow Press, 1984).
6. Arna Bontemps and Jack Conroy, *They Seek a City* (New York: Doubleday, 1945), 217.
7. Imam WD Muhammad, *Ramadan Session* (Homewood, IL, 2003), 4–5.
8. Muhammad, *Ramadan Session*, 9.
9. Imam Ibrahim A. Rahim and Imam Wazir Ali, *The Book of Letters for the Inheritors: An Academic Guide for 21st Century Imams in Support of Imam WD Muhammad*, unpublished manuscript, 2012.
10. Interview with Imam Wallace D. Muhammad (Clifton Marsh, 1984).
11. Edward E. Curtis IV, *Islam in Black America: Identity, Liberation, and Difference in African American Islamic Thought* (New York: State University of New York Press, 2002).
12. Interview, Imam W.D. Mohammed, Chicago, Illinois, July 25, 1979.
13. Don Terry, "W. Deen Mohammed: A Leap of Faith," *Chicago Tribune*, October 20, 2002.
14. Holy Qur'an, Surah Ash-Shura'a, 26:78.
15. Kate Larson, *Bound for the Promised Land: Harriet Tubman, Portrait of an American Hero* (New York: One World Press, 2004).
16. Zaheer Ali, "Return to Roots: The History of Islam in Black America," *Islamic Horizons Magazine* 34, no. 4 (2005): 17–44.
17. Curtis, *Islam in Black America*.
18. *Bilalian News*, November 16, 1979.

19. Imam W. Deen Mohammed, *Mohammed Speaks* (Chicago: WDM Publications, 1999).
20. Brian E. Muhammad, "A New Imam and a New Day of Unity, Cooperation," *Final Call*, July 8, 2013, accessed August 24, 2016, http://www.finalcall.com/artman/publish/National_News_2/article_10048.shtml.
21. WD Muhammad, Lecture given to Muslim World League, April 1977.
22. W. Deen Muhammad, *An African American Genesis* (Chicago: Progressions Publishing, 1986).
23. Elijah Muhammad, "Letter to Abdel Nasser," 1957.
24. Los Angeles, *Herald-Dispatch*, March 12, 1959, I and 5, cited in E. U. Essien-Udom, *Black Nationalism: The Search for an Identity* (Chicago: University of Chicago Press, 1995), 305.
25. Louis Lomax, *When the Word Is Given* (Westport, CT: Greenwood Press, 1963).
26. Lincoln, *Black Muslims in America*.
27. Teresa Watanabe, "Righting Islam's Image in America," *Los Angeles Times*, May 15, 1999.
28. Peter Skerry, "America's Other Muslims," *Wilson Quarterly*, Autumn 2005, http://archive.wilsonquarterly.com/essays/americas-other-muslims.
29. Jackson, *Islam and the Blackamerican*.
30. Sherman Jackson, "Imam W.D. Mohammed and the Third Resurrection," *Marc Manley—Imam at Large* (blog), September 16, 2008, http://www.marcmanley.com/imam-w-d-mohammed-and-the-third-resurrection-by-dr-sherman-jackson/.
31. Shikh Ahmad Kuftaro Foundation, accessed July 23, 2017, http://www.abunour.net/index.php?lan=4.
32. *Muslim Journal*, April 25, 2003.
33. *Muslim Journal*, November 28, 1997.
34. Yehuda Kurtzer, *Shuva: The Future of the Jewish Past* (Waltham, MA: Brandeis University Press, 2012).
35. Steven T. Smith, "An Historical Account of the American Muslim Mission with Specific Reference to North Carolina" (masters thesis, Southeastern Baptist Theological Seminary, 1984), 102; *Muslim Journal*, March 16, 2007; *Muslim Journal*, February 16, 2007.
36. Muqtedar Khan, The Priority of Politics," *Boston Review* (April/May 2003).
37. Shadaab Rahemtulla, *Qur'an of the Oppressed: Liberation Theology and Gender Justice in Islam* (New York: Oxford University Press, 2017); Neil MacFarquhar, "New Translation Prompts Debate on Islamic Verse," *New York Times*. March 25, 2007, accessed August 24, 2016, www.nytimes.com/2007/03/25/us/25koran.html?mcubz=3.
38. W. Deen Mohammed, "Youth Dawa Class (Al Fatiha)," lecture, Chicago, Illinois, October 8, 2001.
39. Bruce Lawrence, *The Qur'an: A Biiography* (New York: Atlantic Monthly Press, 2006), 163–71.
40. W.D. Muhammad, *Imam W. Deen Muhammad Speaks from Harlem, NY: Challenges that Face Man Today*, (Chicago: Zakat Publications, 1988).
41. Surah Zukhruf, 43: 27 and Surah ash Shuraa, 26:78.
42. *Muslim Journal*, September 16, 2011; Darnell Karim "Islamic Studies Materials," accessed July 24, 2917, http://www.islamicstudiesmaterials.com/profile/.
43. Michael V. Perez and Fatima Bahloul, eds., "Imam Warith Deen Mohammed: 'If We Become Independent Thinkers, We Can Make a Contribution,'" *Islamica Magazine*, September 11, 2008, accessed August 24, 2016, http://www.patheos.com/blogs/altmuslim/2008/09/if_we_become_independent_thinkers_we_can_make_a_contribution/.
44. Muhammad, *Al Islam Unity & Leadership*, 85.
45. Ibid., 88.
46. Muhammad, *Ramadan Session*.
47. Ibid., 80–89.
48. Ibid., *Ramadan Sessions*, 10.
49. W. Deen Muhammad, "Justice in Islam: How Close Are We Muslims to Western Democracy?" *Muslim Journal*, August 24, 2001.

50. Muhammad Omar Farooq, *Toward our Reformation: From Legalism to Value-Oriented Islamic Law and Jurisprudence* (Herndon, VA: International Institute of Islamic Thought, 2009).

51. Shahab Ahmed, *What Is Islam: The Importance of Being Islamic* (Princeton, NJ: Princeton University Press, 2016).

Chapter Five

Walking with Brother Imam

The Community of W.D. Mohammed as a Counterweight to Extremism

W.D. Mohammed almost singlehandedly masterminded a pluralistic and nonviolent understanding of Islam rooted in the American experience and, through his influence, created model communities rooted in the Black American Muslim experience. His efforts have given rise to the single largest American community of military veterans, congressmen, doctors, lawyers, and sports and entertainment heroes, as well as ordinary American citizens. This chapter will describe these efforts and provide insights into how other minority Muslim populations in majority non-Muslim societies can remain integrated and productive members of their societies and can serve as a global example to Western and developing countries alike. In no other Western democracy is there a Muslim community that has been in the homeland since the foundation of the nation. As descendants of enslaved Africans, American slavery, and the Jim Crow laws of the American South, Black Americans as a whole and Black American Muslims in particular have inherited a legacy of state violence, racial terrorism, and indiscriminate killing that goes back over a century in American history. However, despite these actions and a difficult history in America, the indigenous Black American Muslim population has remained resilient, with the community of the late W.D. Mohammed setting the example. The community of W.D. Mohammed has not produced a single individual who has been recruited by a domestic or foreign transnational terrorist organization. What has been the formula used that makes this community unique? What has been the focus of W.D. Mohammed's ideology and teachings that has allowed him and his community to get past real and/or perceived grievances and to recognize that their legitimate frustrations had to be channeled via other means? All these questions are legitimate and are at the core of this analysis of what has made W.D. Mohammed's approach so effective.

FORTY-FOUR-YEAR COUNTER-RADICALIZATION PROGRAM

To understand how W.D. Mohammed's efforts were important as a model to serve in other Western democracies and locations throughout the world, we must particularly understand the American context of the Black American Muslim experience. More than fifty years ago, the public perception and dominant framing of Muslims in the public discourse was Black and native-born American. During the 1960s and into the 1970s, "Black Muslims" referred to the indigenous Muslim community in general and the Nation of Islam in particular. However, in the mass American media, this community was dismissed and relegated to being on the margins of society. It was also demonized as being a threat to American and Western values as a result of its radical twist on Islamic concepts and its advocacy for and promotion of Black American liberation theology. Nowhere was this displayed more clearly than in the 1959 television documentary, *The Hate That Hate Produced*, which depicts Elijah Muhammad and his followers as the epitome of hate.[1] In the opening scene, Mike Wallace, the moderator of the show, shares an excerpt of an audio clip of the rhetoric of Malcolm X, then a minister of the Nation of Islam:

> Brothers and sisters, I'm here to tell you that I charge the White man. I charge the White man with being the greatest murderer on earth. I charge the White man with being the greatest kidnapper on earth. There is no place in this world that that man can go and say he created peace and harmony. Everywhere he's gone he's created havoc. Everywhere he's gone he's created destruction. So I charge him. I charge him with being the greatest kidnapper on this earth. I charge him with being the greatest murderer on this earth. I charge him with being the greatest robber and enslaver on this earth. I charge the White man with being the greatest swine-eater on this earth, the greatest drunkard on this earth.
>
> He can't deny the charges. You can't deny the charges. We're the living proof of those charges. You and I are the proof. You're not an American, you are the victim of America. You didn't have a choice coming over here. He didn't say, "Black man, Black woman, come on over and help me build America." He said, "Nigger, get down in the bottom of that boat and I'm taking you over there to help me build America." Being born here does not make you an American. I'm not an American. You're not an American. You are one of twenty-two million Black people who are the victims of America.
>
> You and I, we've never seen any democracy. We ain't seen no democracy in the cotton fields of Georgia. That wasn't no democracy down there. We

didn't see any democracy on the streets of Harlem and the streets of Brooklyn and the streets of Detroit and Chicago. That wasn't democracy down there. No, we've never seen democracy; all we've seen is hypocrisy. We don't see any American dream. We've experienced only the American nightmare.[2]

In the show, Mike Wallace seeks to delegitimize the Black Muslim identity by framing the practices of the community of the Nation of Islam as hateful. This image was presented in contrast to that of orthodox Muslim practices and overseas Muslims, who were generally portrayed as acceptable and within the mainstream. All of this is quite interesting in the broader context, given that the later immigrant Muslim community had not yet arrived in America. (The Immigration and Nationality Acts of 1952 and 1965 brought large influxes of Arabs and Southeast Asians to the United States.) It stands in stark contrast to the contemporary perspective of Muslims as being synonymous with Arab and foreign.

W.D. Mohammed instituted revisions to his father's teachings to introduce mainstream Islamic concepts to the rank-and-file members of the former Nation of Islam. I would argue that, within the lessons and catechism of the Nation of Islam, the mythology and false creation narrative provided a protection from immigrant and foreign interpretations of Islam. In fact, in his supreme lessons, Elijah Muhammad presented a compilation of dos and don'ts to make sure his communities were staying insular and not introducing outside forces and elements. Though rooted in black nationalism and separatist ideals, this strategic decision—which was, by default, continued by W.D. Mohammed—has in some way created a buffer that allows communities to reject, denounce, and chart out a new pathway away from foreign and immigrant interpretations of Islam, thereby creating a formula of resistance against elements like violent extremism.[3] The outward rejection of Islamism, a political ideology that promotes a narrow, rigid interpretation of Islam using the umbrella of Islamic solidarity, was one that Elijah Muhammad and W.D. Mohammed both rejected outright. Elijah Muhammad made it clear, stating, "Neither Jeddah or Mecca have sent me! I am sent from Allah and not from the Secretary General of the Muslim League," referring to the Muslim World League, a pan-Islamic organization that was established in 1962 to govern the broader Muslim world.[4] The cultural anthropologist Reinhold Loeffler provides a compelling argument as to how we can analyze W.D. Mohammed's community and its particularistic version of Islam that has aided in its resistance to extremism and in its formation of an American Islam. Loeffler observed the following:

> An amazing variety of individual world views in a single, rather homogenous village.... In this small village, Islam can take the form of a bland legalism of a consuming devotion to the good of others; an ideology legitimizing established status and power or a critical theology challenging the very status and

power; a devotive quietism or fervent zealotism; an -osity or humble trust in God's compassion; a rigid fundamentalism or reformist modernism; a ritualism steeped in folklore and magic or a scriptural purism. . . .

Confronted with such fundamental diversity, we have to discard any essentialist conception of Islam. Instead, Islam has to be understood as the totality of all symbolic forms considered Islamic by people regarding themselves as Muslims; i.e. an essentiality unbounded complex of symbols and principles which on most any issue offer a wide range of possible, even opposing conceptions, meanings, attitudes and modes of thought, each formulated with sufficient fluidity to allow ever more spinoffs, elaborations and interpretations. . . .

But this material teaches us also not to overlook the subjectivity of the individual believer. For Muslims, theologian, scholar, or layman alike, God can speak but with one tongue. Consequently, there can only be one true Islam, and that is usually the believers' own. What we perceive as diversity, for the believer is a matter of right and wrong. Thus, while we acknowledge the various Islamic forms—African, Arabian, Indonesian; traditionalist, modernist, fundamentalist—as equally authentic expressions of Islam, we also have to acknowledge that in this sea of diversity each believer upholds his form as the only really true one.[5]

W.D. Mohammed's decision to frame Islam and Black identity as a whole in an American context was part of what has made his efforts so unique. Dr. Sherman Jackson, in his book *Islam and the Blackamerican* captures these points in the following passage:

The perennial problem for Black Americans have against the dreaded threats of assimilationism, domination, and cultural apostasy. In this light, the perennial problem for Black Americans—Muslims and non-Muslim alike—has been how to embrace ways and institutions that are identified with the dominant culture without violating one's sense of agency and authentic self. This is what the early Black American proto-Islamic movements understood so well. Their alternative modalities of American blackness were at once functionally pragmatic and virulently anti-assimilationist. This presented Black Americans not only with the opportunity to escape the negative definitions of blackness imposed by the dominant culture but also to embrace in good conscience aspects of the collective American heritage that prepared them for a dignified social, economic, and political existence. This was an alternative modality of American blackness that not only rejected the inherent superiority of whiteness but also highlighted and took aim against the most egregious pathologies and dysfunctionalities of the urban ghetto. Wanton hedonism, the glorification of ignorance, victimology, and the dereliction of traditional duties of manhood gave way to thrift, discipline, social etiquette, and education as essential features of any self-respecting "black man."[6]

By offering another approach to Islamic dogma, W.D. Mohammed and his ancestral community have been able to stand firmly on solid ground to resist the appeal of Islamist hegemony and foreign Islam that has been popularized throughout the world. My assumption in this book is that W.D. Mohammed was very aware of the impact that foreign influence, whether good or bad, could have on his impressionable community. By creating independent approaches to combat this transnational appeal that has gained a strong foothold in the contemporary era, W.D. Mohammed has offered some tangible solutions to our present-day issues of religious radicalism.[7]

By offering a third option away from the American mainstream but still within mainstream American idealism, W.D. Mohammed sought to keep alive the positive aspects of his father's views, such as self-respect, but pushed hard to establish them on the basis of orthodox Islam as filtered through the Black American experience. At the center of W.D. Mohammed's reform efforts is the theme of redemption and the perception of divine intervention in the affairs of Black American life. It is this theme that fostered his community's ability to withstand the difficulties that had affected and continue to affect Black Americans. Timur Yuskaev, a scholar of contemporary Islam and author of the upcoming book *Speaking Qur'an: The Emergence of an American Sacred Text,* has highlighted how the redemption rhetoric of W.D. Mohammed's community and the religious theology of the Nation of Islam served to connect these two organizations with the broader aspects of Black American religion as a whole. This connection is what is C. Eric Lincoln and Lawrence Mamiya have termed the "black sacred cosmos."[8] According to Yuskaev, these authors use this term to describe Black Americans' articulation of both visual and religious motifs along with their meanings for the purpose of explaining the Black American religious experience. This point is further amplified in Mahmoud Ayoub's analysis of redemption in his work *Redemptive Suffering in Islam:*

> Redemption is used here in its broadest sense to mean the healing of existence or the fulfillment of human life. . . . This fulfillment through suffering is what this study will call redemption. This basic assumption is that all suffering can, in some sense, be regarded as redemptive where faith is present; the faith which gives hope against despair and fulfillment against the annihilation of death.[9]

For W.D. Mohammed, this theme of redemption offered a way for Black Americans to experience a form of deliverance and healing in the aftermath of their challenging experiences in America. He illustrated this as follows:

> Now we are balancing (Elijah Muhammad's teachings) so we can develop an awareness in the children (of Islam) that they are not only members of a race but they are citizens—members of a nation—we want to grow in the full dimension of our country . . . my greatest desire for our community AMM [American Muslim Mission, one of the many names that WD Muhammad named his community] is to . . . one day hear that a Muslim, a real Muslim, a

genius Muslim from our Community has become a governor, or a senator, or head of some big American corporation.[10]

This point highlighted by W.D. Mohammed would come to be showcased by the elections of Keith Ellison of Minnesota in 2006 and Andre Carson of Indiana in 2008 to the House of Representatives. Both men were exposed to the insights and leadership of W.D. Mohammed, and both continue to be strong supporters of his community.[11]

Finally, flagship educational institutions within the W.D. Mohammed community, connected to more than 300 mosques throughout the United States, including the W.D. Mohammed high school in Atlanta, have served as an important model for the community's emphasis on preserving its legacy and model into the future. In educational institutions like the Mohammed Schools of Atlanta, which serve children from third to twelfth grade, the mission is to "teach all students to accept their G-d given responsibilities and full potential, as we provide a nurturing environment that engages students in discovery and critical thinking."[12] This framework has, for forty-two years, provided an American Muslim methodological approach that has worked to teach Muslims the spirit of the Qur'an and the life example of Muhammad, and it neither condones resentment toward the West nor teaches Muslims to reject their American culture.

Instead, it challenges the community to become productive, tolerant, and open members of society at large, wherever they live.

RESILIENCE STRATEGIES

In the wake of terrorist attacks in Nice, Orlando, Istanbul, Dhaka, Kabul, and other cities throughout the globe, public awareness campaigns are more essential than ever to address the threat of violent extremism. The increase in the number of attacks by Daesh and other transnational terrorist groups and the sophistication and diversification of their TTPs (techniques, tactics, and procedures) have demonstrated these groups' adaptability and proven that local communities are more vulnerable to terrorist attacks than ever before.

The White House Countering Violent Extremism (CVE) summit in 2015, together with follow-up meetings and the January 2016 publication of the UN Secretary General's Action Plan to Prevent Violent Extremism, served in many ways to rally the international community toward high-level support for a swift response involving private sector, civil society, religious, and government participants. And in May 2017, the State Department and United States Agency for International Development (USAID) released their first-ever Joint Strategy on Countering Violent Extremism to help communities identify the early signs of radicalization and intervene before violence begins. Countries all over the world, including Kenya, Nigeria, Pakistan, and the United States, are pulling together national CVE strategies in an effort to come up with tailored responses based on each country's specific demands and needs in order to steer citizens away from a path of radicalization.

The emergence of a new breed of violent extremist groups throughout the world has been felt domestically, with new recruits being driven by international conflict as well as domestic change, and the increase in individuals being radicalized and mobilized in the United States has raised concern among local populations. In January 2016, Joshua Skule, assistant director of intelligence at the Washington Field Office of the Federal Bureau of Investigation, stated, "When we look at the threat reporting emanating from ISIL and other [homegrown violent extremists] around the country, we know there is a constant and persistent threat to the District of Columbia." A 2017 open-source report of a Department of Homeland Security intelligence assessment found that most foreign-born violent extremists did not arrive in the United States radicalized, but rather became radicalized after living in the United States for several years. Counterterrorism experts are increasingly using the internet, specifically social media, to monitor and contest the space of violent extremists with mixed results. However, these efforts are often undertaken without the guidance of reputable American Islamic scholars or Muslim educators, psychologists, sociologists, family members, or former violent extremists who have a deeper understanding of Islamic extremism.

Resilience is the ability of a community, people, state, or region to adopt new processes, norms, and strategies for conducting their lives and to build new societal relationships in order to prevent, mitigate, or recover from a violent shock or uptick in aggression and brutality. In both academic and public policy circles, the concept of resilience in response to a shock or a long-term stressful event is characterized by a systems approach, meaning it should be viewed at both a macro- and a microlevel. In the larger context, it is a broader community resilience that occurs when people are confronted with the threat of violent extremism. In her investigation of resilience work in Kenya, Lauren Van Metre, formerly with the US Institute of Peace, provides analysis into what makes communities resilient in the face of transnational terrorism and state violence. This work builds on the research of Ashutosh Varshney into community resilience in reaction to communal violence in India as well as Ami Carpenter's analysis of the resilience of Baghdad communities to sectarian violence and Marshall Wallace and Mary Anderson's comparative analysis of nonwar communities.[13] These collective bodies of work have built upon each other to provide compelling new insights into the subject, especially in light of geographic location. According to Lauren Van Metre,

> All three studies note the importance of bridging relationships among diverse community groups in preventing or mitigating violence and collective effica-

cy, or a community's belief that it has the power to achieve shared goals. Wallace and Anderson make a special contribution in the area of leadership; they identify the importance of specific leadership styles. Carpenter identifies the crucial role of "overlapping" ties, or relationships community groups have with groups outside their community. Sectarian groups entered Baghdad communities through familial relations between rural and urban tribes. In aggregating their findings, this study tests a framework for community resilience to violent extremism.[14]

For Van Metre, resilience does not refer to the restoration of the status quo but rather to learning and adaptation. In the case of W.D. Mohammed, his ability to offer options for channeling real and perceived grievances in ways that utilized people's constitutional rights, and thus encourage his community's resilience, provides an example of how to combat the cyclical nature of violence. For Black American communities as a whole, the exposure to communal and state violence goes back to the period during and immediately following America's inception, a time when they were subjected to violence and terrorism on a large scale and how early Black Americans sought to survive and exist in the midst of difficult conditions.[15]

The systems approach described above has made major inroads within public policy circles in Washington. A number of government agencies have produced reports in this area. In particular, in 2013, the USAID published *A Framework for Analyzing Resilience in Fragile and Conflict-Affected States*.[16] Rather than focusing on individual and group levels of analysis, this paper took a systems approach, hypothesizing that five types of external shocks (economic, environmental, security, political, and social) interact with one another and with three bases of community resilience (institutions, resources, and adaptive facilitators) to produce systemic outcomes. This framework helps bridge the "levels of analysis" problem and illuminates the complexity of resilience, because "instead of detailing a linear cause and effect relationship, the complex systems approach examines the influence/impact of interacting factors in response to a shock or stress."[17] Although there are various pathways on the road to extremism for individuals, groups, and communities, a systems approach helps illuminate the varying risk and resilience factors in particular situations.

RESILIENCE TO VIOLENCE

As Van Metre has offered, analysis of resilience to violence are not new, but they are limited. This study builds off three previous frameworks for community resilience to violence, those of Ashutosh Varshney in *Ethnic Conflict and Civic Life: Hindus and Muslims in India*, Ami Carpenter in *Community*

Resilience to Sectarian Violence in Baghdad, and Marshall Wallace and Mary Anderson in *Opting Out of War*.

In his seminal work on the relationship between the structure of civil society and the outbreak of ethnic violence in India, Varshney studies six cities by dividing them into three pairs according to similar ethnic makeup and analyzing why one community within each pair remained peaceful while the other did not after experiencing an exogenous shock. His conclusion is that the cities with institutionalized peace systems could absorb such shocks without outbreaks of communal violence. While Varshney's study does not explicitly focus on resilience, his conceptual framework—examining the ability of "peace" systems in India to absorb shocks such as urban riots—does relate closely to the formulation of resilience and adaptive systems. An important component of community resilience to violence is preexisting local networks of civic engagement among ethnic groups. Associational forms of civic engagement (that is, organized networks bound together by working trust across ethnic groups, such as business associations, labor unions, organized clubs, etc.) are more resilient to violence than intercommunal quotidian, or daily associations, such as interactions at markets, soccer games, or festivals.

In Carpenter's appraisal of the sectarian conflict in Baghdad, she identifies a multitier framework for conflict resilience: (1) regime characteristics—"the strengths and abilities of a system that enable it to respond adaptively to change" and (2) community competence—"the ability of a system to modify or change characteristics or behavior to cope better with actual or anticipated stresses."[18]

The articulations captured by Van Metre, Varshney, Carpenter, and others provide a framework for us all to collectively learn from how communities and societies can find effective approaches to combat extremism. In the case of W.D. Mohammed, his resilience mechanism of fusing American patriotism, Islamic religious dogma, black empowerment, and black social upliftment techniques were efforts that have proven to be effective for his community.

EXTREMIST RECRUITMENT IN THE AFRICAN AMERICAN MUSLIM COMMUNITY

Transnational terrorists have always seen the African American Muslim community as grounds for potential recruits. African American Muslim encounters with overseas Muslims, largely from the Arab world and Southeast Asia, have been documented going back to the 1940s and 1950s.[19] In the mid-1980s and 1990s, Muslims in the United States, particularly African American Muslims, were actively recruited to fight in the Afghan jihad to expel the USSR, supported by the US government.[20] Additionally, missionary activities starting in the early 1990s coincided with a period of large influxes of cash from the Arabian Peninsula and the reawakening of African American social identity.[21] In America, the epicenters of East Orange, New Jersey, and Philadelphia, Pennsylvania, became the locations for vibrant missionary activities, which provided lucrative educational scholarships, and satellite exchanges with Saudi-based clerics and immediate cash into urban communities who were desperate for resources. These efforts prompted the emergence of African American Salafi[22] clerics who became emissaries of Salafi thought and provided tremendous influence for conversion.

After the election of Barack Obama in 2008, Ayman al Zawahiri (then second in command of al-Qa'ida) sought to interlace domestic African American racial grievances with the global jihad movement in a video message.[23] In this message, Zawahiri presented video motifs of Malcolm X, attempting to exploit historical African American Muslim activism as a potential means for future radicalization and mobilization. This effort was judged to be largely unsuccessful.[24]

In summer 2015, the al-Qa'ida published a six-page feature piece titled, "The Blacks in America," which outlined the historical injustices and atrocities inflicted on African slaves upon their arrival in America to the incidences of violence inflicted on youth in urban cities throughout the United States. Equally important, the authors of the article sought to connect Islamic historical events with that of the plight of the current state of African Americans, particularly that of Bilal, an Ethiopian convert to Islam, and the brutality he faced in the early days of Islam.

In the same year, the Islamic State (ISIS) published an article titled "Wala and Bara versus American Racism" in issue 11 of their now-defunct *DABIQ* magazine. In the article, English-language propagators of the extremist organization used Qur'anic text to provide justification and rationale to denounce American racism, while using narrations of the Prophet Muhammad to call on African Americans to embrace Islam and see the colorblindness of the Islamic State's ummah.[25] Their desire to connect with African Americans as a whole, particularly with African American Muslims, should be seen as an overall attempt by the organization to be keenly aware of ways to create fissures within American's minority populations.

According to the New America Foundation database, roughly 12 percent of the terrorist recruits in America have been Black Americans.[26] Most recently in 2019, thirty-four-year-old Texan native Warren Christopher Clark traveled to northern Syria and was being held by Kurdish authorities for his support of ISIS, and during an interview with Western media, he said, "I wanted to go see exactly what the group was about, and what they were doing." In 2018, Demetrius Nathaniel Pitts was arrested in Cleveland, Ohio, for his plan to attack Fourth of July festivities on behalf of ISIS. In 2017,

Tairod Pugh, a former US Air Force veteran, was convicted for attempting to join ISIS and sentenced in a New Jersey court to thirty-five years in prison.[27] In 2016, Gregory Hubbard, Dayne Antani Christian, and Darren Arness Jackson, all from Albany, Georgia, were arrested and charged for plotting to go to Syria and train on behalf of ISIS to carry out terror plots inside the United States.[28] In 2015, Elton Simpson went to Garland, Texas, to kill organizers of a Prophet Muhammad cartoon contest on behalf of ISIS.[29] In 2014, Douglas McArthur McCain was considered one of the first Americans to die fighting for ISIS, and Alton Nolen used a knife to viciously behead a co-worker at Vaughn Foods in Oklahoma.[30] In the case of all the Black Americans described here and others who traveled on behalf of al-Qaida and ISIS, none have been affiliated with the W.D. Mohammed community. In the case of community resilience, the W.D. Mohammed community provides compelling examples of how efforts can be made to resist violent tendencies. W.D. Mohammed's methodical community approach, experience in and out of nationalistic and religious fundamentalism over decades, and openness to American society, culture, and politics have set its parishioners and members apart from other communities as a whole. His approach of supporting group pride, race consciousness, and independence, all while embracing Americanness, has served him and his community in a unique way.

NOTES

1. Mike Wallace, *The Hate That Hate Produced* office memo. United States government document July 17, 1959, accessed July 28, 2017, http://www.columbia.edu/cu/ccbh/mxp/pdf/071659hthp-transcript.pdf.

2. Ibid.

3. Fard Muhammad, "The Supreme Wisdom Lessons," *The Lost Found Nation of Islam in North America*, accessed on July 27, 2017, https://www.scribd.com/document/10047804/The-Supreme-Wisdom-Lessons.

4. "Mr. Muhammad Answers Critics: Authority from Allah None Other," *Muhammad Speaks*, August 2, 1962, 3.

5. Reinhold Loeffler, *Islam in Practice: Religious Beliefs in a Persian Village* (Albany: State University of New York Press, 1988), 246–47.

6. Jackson, *Islam and the Blackamerican*, 156–57.

7. Ahmed, *What is Islam: The Importance of Being Islamic*.

8. Timur Yuskaev, "Redeeming the Nation: Redemption Theology in African American Islam," *Studies in Contemporary Islam* 1, no. 1 (1999): 29–61.

9. Mahmoud Ayoub, *Redemptive Suffering in Islam: A Study of the Devotional Aspects of Ashura in Twelver Shi'ism* (The Hague: Morton Publishers, 1978), 23.

10. Dirk Sager, "Communicating for Survival," interview, Station ZDF, German Television, *World Community of Islam*, news release, December 27, 1979.

11. "Keith Ellison and Andre Carson Discuss Donald Trump's Rhetoric on Muslims," C-Span.org, May 24, 2016.

12. WD Mohammed Schools of Atlanta, accessed July 27, 2017, http://mohammedschools.org.

13. Ashutosh Varshney, *Ethnic Conflict and Civic Life: Hindus and Muslims in India* (New Haven, CT: Yale University Press, 2002); Ami C. Carpenter, *Community Resilience to Sectarian Violence in Baghdad* (New York: Springer, 2014); and Mary B. Anderson and Marshall

Wallace, *Opting Out of War: Strategies to Prevent Violent Conflict* (Boulder, CO: Lynne Rienner, 2012).

14. Lauren Van Metre, "Peacebuilding and Resilience," U.S. Institute of Peace, 2016.

15. Charles M. Blow, "Black Men, Violence and 'Fierce Urgency,'" *The New York Times*, May 5, 2016, accessed August 24, 2016, https://www.nytimes.com/2016/05/05/opinion/black-men-violence-and-fierce-urgency.html?mcubz=3.

16. Alejandra Bujones, Katrin Jaskiewicz, Lauren Linakis, and Michael McGirr, "A Framework for Analyzing Resilience in Fragile and Conflict-Affected Situations," School of International and Public Affairs, Columbia University, Washington, DC, Presentation for USAID, November 23, 2014, accessed August 24, 2016, https://sipa.columbia.edu/sites/default/files/USAID%20Final%20Report.pdf.

17. Ibid., 7.

18. Carpenter, *Community Resilience to Sectarian Violence in Baghdad*, 76.

19. Los Angeles, *Herald-Dispatch*, March 12, 1959, I and 5, cited in Essien-Udom, *Black Nationalism: The Search for an Identity*, 305.

20. See "Today's Terrorism Didn't Start with 9/11—It Dtarted with the '90s," CNN, August 2, 2017, accessed September 19, 2017, www.cnn.com/2017/08/02/opinions/nineties-terrorism-bergen/index.html.

21. Jennings, *Blacks, Latinos and Asians in Urban America*: Yuri Kochiyama, *The Impact of Malcolm X on Asian-American Politics and Activism*.

22. We describe African American Salafism as those practitioners who seek to follow the way and example of Muhammad using a literal reading of the Qur'an. Many adherents are conservative in their orientation, synonymous to southern Baptists in the American South being conservative. In no way is Salafism equated directly to extremism. Instead, adherents seek to adopt a life of mostly literalism, but who seek to find a way to apply these religious values in the twenty-first century.

23. See "Third Interview with Dr. Ayman al-Zawahiri—5/2007," May 5, 2007, accessed September 13, 2017 https://archive.org/details/Third-Interview.

24. See "Al Qaeda Leader Mocks Obama in Web Posting," CNN, November 19, 2008, accessed September 13, 2017, www.cnn.com/2008/US/11/19/obama.alqaeda/.

25. "From the Battle of Al-Ahzab, to the War of Coalitions, Wala and Bara versus American Racism," *Dabiq Magazine*, no. 11 (2015): 18. (Islamic Calendar) Dhul Q'adah, 1436 (2015).

26. New America Foundation, accessed July 28, 2017, https://www.newamerica.org.

27. Joseph Goldstein, "Tairod Pugh, Ex-U.S. Serviceman, Is Found Guilty of Trying to Aid ISIS," *New York Times*, March 9, 2016.

28. Jane Musgrave, "Lake Park Man Pleads Guilty to Trying to Help ISIS," *Palm Beach Post*, accessed July 27, 2017: http://www.palmbeachpost.com/news/crime--law/new-lake-park-man-pleads-guilty-trying-help-isis/ZSNaFgWr2pw0K8wMdXgsRO/.

29. Holly Yan, "Texas Attack: What We Know about Elton Simpson and Nadir Soofi," May 5, 2015, accessed July 27, 2017, http://www.cnn.com/2015/05/05/us/texas-shooting-gunmen/index.html .

30. Sonia Moghe, Holly Yan, and Greg Botelho, "Douglas Arthur McCain: From American Kid to Jihadi in Syria," September 3, 2014, accessed July 27, 2017, http://www.cnn.com/2014/08/27/us/who-was-douglas-mccain/index.html.

Conclusion

Beginning with a description of the role of Islamic identity in West Africa and its journey to America, I have sought to discuss the emergence of an American Islam that fuses together Islamic orthodoxy, Black Nationalism, spirituality, and the impact of American Protestantism as well as elements from the continental West African Islamic revivalist tradition. This work is unique in its focus on the American Muslim revivalist Imam W.D. Mohammed and its demonstration of the continuum of the Islamic revivalist tradition that originated in West African Islamic institutions.

By situating W.D. Mohammed in the position of an American Islamic revivalist, we are able to see his contribution to the religious and cultural discourse of American, Islamic, and Black thought and how it connects the Islamic intellectual contributions of West Africa with those of the larger Islamic world. For future research in this field, I am reminded of the legacy of the influence of the Nation of Islam and W.D. Mohammed at-large community perspectives that could serve as some interesting entry points in how the communities coreligionists might learn from the community's experience. For example, the former paramilitary division of the Nation of Islam, known as the Fruit of Islam, served as a protective internal security arm. It has loosely carried its way into W.D. Mohammed's circles, without the structure and rigidity of the former movement, as an effort to ensure that women, children, and the elderly continue to be protected.

For other global communities, including Muslim ones, there might be good lessons to take from this example. This type of chivalry education for young men—known in Japanese society as *bushido, futuwwa* in the Arab world, and formerly in the West, *paideia*—might offer some compelling ways in which young, disaffected, and susceptible populations might be able to channel their frustrations into useful and practical religious and social means. Efforts like this, along with arts, culture, and certainly the community model instituted by W.D. Mohammed, provide ways from which American Muslims and the global Muslim community can learn in the present and the future in combatting violent extremism. W.D. Mohammed, I argue, offered something rather revolutionary by developing a new way of thinking and independence based on the American experience, while using a Qur'anic logic that allowed himself and his community to avoid the extremist thinking and views of other communities by recognizing his experience in the Untied States. W.D. Mohammed captures this succinctly in the August 1985 edition of *Progressions* magazine:

> The African-American is a race distinguished in America from other races, and is also a minority group in this country. As far as the courts and healthy minded people of this country are concerned, we are as welcome here as any other citizen. Our right to be a citizen has been won, but we still have to fight, to struggle for a comfortable place in this society if we are to prosper and grow strong.
>
> The African-American represents a threat to most independent minded ethnic groups in America. We pose a threat because we are uncomfortable with ourselves and un-established as a race, and as a community. A person who is unhappy at home will sometimes run to someone else's house, and that is what many African-Americans do because they are not happy in their own communities. You might think other ethnic groups are not entitled to their own separate community in America, but that is incorrect.
>
> America is a pluralistic society. Other ethnic groups should be left alone to live their own cultural life in their own neighborhoods, and we should not try to destroy the character of those neighborhoods because this is America.
>
> What I am saying to African-Americans is what the white man feels in his heart but won't say. It would put him in a very uncomfortable position. He believes that if he said these things to us, it would hurt our feelings and bring up old thoughts, and he hates to bring up old thoughts. His hands are tied. He can't be honest with us in a conversation. But thank God, we can be honest with each other. . . .
>
> I know these truths about ourselves leaves a hurt feeling, but a truthful person can be in control of their feelings. If someone tells a lie, it is not going to hurt the truthful person. Lies only hurt a liar. As a people, we have a way of lying to ourselves and others. We think that we have to prove something to outsiders, and we are constantly trying to do just that. We have been in this habit so long that it has become natural for us.
>
> Most of our people want to carry the personality and spiritual makeup that we think outsiders will approve. But before you think about outsiders, you should first think about your family. You should first want to be accepted by your family. You should want your family to approve of how you feel, how you think, and how you are motivated. Your behavior should be determined by the home situation. If you can form the behavior that is good for yourself, your family, your relatives and closest associates, then you can go anywhere in this world and people will accept you. But when people see you trying to satisfy

outsiders, and you are not conscious of the need to satisfy your own people, they find it hard to accept you. If you won't be true to your own people at home, they will reason that you won't be true to anybody else, and they will be correct.

This pretense on the part of most African-Americans to satisfy outsiders is a lie; it is false, and we must face up to this truth even though it is uncomfortable to many of us. We must remind ourselves that this is America, and we have the same right to establish our own ethnic dignity as any other race or group in this society. We don't need to prove anything to anybody if we would just be true to ourselves.[1]

POLICY NEXUS

For the US, Western, and global policy makers throughout the world, countering violent extremism strategies that employ some of the techniques offered by W.D. Mohammed offer compelling solutions that can be innovative, adaptive, and local that best addresses the needs of their environment. The slow but purposeful strategy of W.D. Mohammed in particular showed an individual and a community who wrestled with the real grievances of past state violence and actions and, in many ways, the struggle between the struggle to reconcile the divisive rhetoric of the Nation of Islam but also its role it has played to radically reform Black Americans to express religion, their identity, and freedom of religious thought on their own terms. All these efforts can serve as an option for US policy makers to engage communities like these who might consider engaging Black American Muslim imams, their students, and ideological teachings that have served as quiet and critical voices in the fight against extremism and might offer one antidote approaches out of many in soft power approaches.

NOTE

1. W.D. Muhammad, *Progressions*, August 1985.

Glossary of Terms

African American Islam: Islam as practiced by descendants of enslaved Africans and indigenous-born African Americans who converted to normative Islam as a form of protest against slavery and who seek to claim their Islamic heritage and future trajectory as American-born Muslims.

Bismillah: An invocation of God's name and part of the beginning of the opening chapter of the Qur'an.

Brother Imam: The title given to the late W.D. Mohammed by his followers. This use of terminology conveys a sense of equality among men and women who consider him their leader while appropriately giving him the respect and honor as the religious leader of the community.

Credible Voice: Any influential figure who can undercut the appeal of violent extremists with a specific audience.

Din: Arabic word for religion in Islam.

Fiqh: Islamic jurisprudence as implemented in society.

Hijrah: An Islamic concept meaning migration. It is often used by individuals to describe leaving one location for another in search of knowledge and spiritual discovery. Extremists have used the term to encourage Americans to leave the their homeland and travel to places like Syria and Iraq to support their causes.

Islam: The religion of 1.5 billion adherents who call themselves Muslims; it comes from the Arabic root word that means peace.

Jihad: Literally, the Arabic word meaning "to strive" or "to struggle." It can have an internal and an external meaning of the act of striving to be a good

Muslim or the personal challenges that an individual may or may not face (i.e., vices, behavior choices, etc.). The modern-day concept of jihad has largely been used to connote warfare, due to extremist groups, but most mainstream Islamic scholars highlight that there are numerous conditions for this to even be necessary.

Kufr: Someone who disbelieves in God's teachings. Largely, extremist groups use this concept as a litmus test against moderate Muslims who reject the extremist and fringe interpretations of terrorist groups and, as a result, are deemed *kufr* by extremist jurists.

Madhab: School of Islamic jurisprudence.

Madrasa: A place of study; a formal school in which Qur'anic religious instruction historically and contemporarily is conducted.

Radicalization: The process by which individuals adopt a set of beliefs and impose it on others through the use of violence in order to achieve social and political change.

Salafi-Jihadi: A strict interpretation of Islam that is literalist in its approach and advocates for violence and armed combat for all Muslims. Its origins are rooted in Wahhabi teachings based in Saudi Arabia and are considered outside mainstream Muslim circles of influence. The groups ISIS, Al-Qa'ida, Boko Haram, and Al-Shabaab subscribe to these beliefs.

Sufism: The mystical and spiritual dimension in Islam; similar to some of the mystical traditions in Christianity (i.e., Catholic traditions of the Benedictine and Franciscan orders or Pentecostal traditions) and Kabbalism in Judaism.

Sunna: The way of Muhammad, the founder of Islam, via his actions, conducts, and beliefs. This concept is similar to the Christian understanding of the example of Jesus Christ, whose good behavior close disciples sought to emulate.

Takfir: The acts of excommunication or apostasy in Islam. In the modern age, extremist groups use this term to describe largely mainstream Muslims who disagree with their tactics.

Taqiyyah: The concept of hiding one's religious beliefs and practices so as to avoid persecution or physical harm. This practice has been followed in some Islamic traditions throughout history and largely implemented in Shia traditions. This term is often used as a sign of respect toward elder imams who followed his leadership upon his death.

Ummah: Arabic term meaning community and oftentimes used to represent the local and international community of Muslims.

Violent Extremist: A person who advocates, is engaged in, or is preparing to engage in ideologically motivated terrorist activities (including providing support to terrorism) in furtherance of political or social objectives promoted by a foreign terrorist organization. This term includes violent extremists acting inside the United States.

Wird: Devotion or liturgy specific to a Sufi order. It involves specialized prayers in which the Sufi order is defined, usually through Qur'anic passages or Arabic prayers as created by the founder of the order. The initiate of the order is given the secret wird of the order upon completion of the training, thus transferring the spiritual power of the chain of transmission from the founder of the order and Muhammad to the initiate.

Zawiyah: A religious hostel for Sufi practitioners.

Bibliography

PRIMARY SOURCES

Newspapers and Periodicals (various dates)

Bilalian News (Chicago)
Charleston City Gazette (Charleston, SC)
Charleston State Gazette of South Carolina
Charleston Times (Charleston, SC)
Chicago Defender
Columbian Herald
Moorish Voice (Chicago)
Moslem Sunrise (Chicago)
Muhammad Speaks (Chicago)
Muslim Journal (Chicago)
New York Amsterdam News
New York Times

SECONDARY SOURCES

Abdi, Cawo M. *Elusive Jannah: The Somali Diaspora and a Borderless Muslim Identity.* Minneapolis: University of Minnesota Press, 2015.

Abdullah, Zain. *Black Mecca: The African Muslims of Harlem.* New York: Oxford University Press, 2010.

Abdullah, Zain. "Negotiating Identities: A History of Islamization in Black West Africa." *Journal of Islamic Law and Culture* 10, no. 1 (2008): 5–18.

Abdullah, Zain. "Sufis on Parade: The Performance of Black, African, and Muslim Identities." *Journal of the American Academy of Religion* 77, no. 2 (2009): 199–237.

Abdul-Matin, Ibrahim. *Green Deen: What Islam Teaches about Protecting the Planet.* San Francisco, CA: Berrett Koehler, 2010.

Bibliography

Abdul-Rauf, Muhammad. *Bilal ibn Rabah: A Leading Companion of the Prophet Muhammad.* Indianapolis, IN: American Trust Publications, 1977.

Abun-Nasr, Jamil. *The Tijaniyya: A Sufi Order in the Modern World.* New York: Oxford University Press, 1965.

Afroz, Sultana. "From Moors to Marronage: The Islamic Heritage of the Maroons in Jamaica." *Journal of Muslim Minority Affairs* 19, no. 2 (1999): 161–79.

Afroz, Sultana. "Invisible Yet Invincible: The Muslim Ummah in Jamaica." *Journal of Muslim Minority Affairs* 23, no. 1 (2003): 211–22.

Afroz, Sultana. "The Role of Islam in the Abolition of Slavery and in the Development of British Capitalism." *American Journal of Islamic Social Sciences* 29, no. 1, (2012): 1–29.

Ahmed, Shahab. *What Is Islam: The Importance of Being Islamic.* Princeton, NJ: Princeton University Press, 2016.

Ahmed, Sumayya. "Islam Is a Black American." ISLAMiCommentary, December 11, 2015. Accessed August 24, 2016, http://islamicommentary.org/2015/12/islam-is-a-black-american-by-sumayya-ahmed/.

Aidi, Hisham. "Jihadis in the Hood: Race, Urban Islam and the War on Terror." *Middle East Research and Information Project.* Accessed August 24, 2016. http://www.merip.org/mer/mer224/jihadis-hood.

Aidi, Hisham. "'Let Us Be Moors': Islam, Race and 'Connected Histories.'" *Middle East Research and Information Project.* Accessed August 24, 2016. http://www.merip.org/mer/mer229/let-us-be-moors.

Aidi, Hisham. *Rebel Music: Race, Empire and the New Muslim Youth Culture.* New York: Pantheon Books, 2014.

Ajrouch, Kristine J., and Abdi M. Kusow. "Racial and Religious Contexts: Situational Identities among Lebanese and Somali Muslim Immigrants." *Ethnic and Racial Studies* 30, no. 1 (2007): 72–94.

Akande, Habeeb. *Illuminating the Blackness: Blacks and African Muslims in Brazil.* London: Rabaah Publishers, 2016.

Akande, Habeeb. *Illuminating the Darkness: Blacks and North Africans in Islam.* London: Rabaah Publishers, 2012.

Al-Ahari, Muhammad A. *Bilali Muhammad: Muslim Jurisprudist in Antebellum Georgia.* Chicago: Magribine Press, 2010.

Al-Ahari, Muhammad A., ed. *Five Classic Muslim Slave Narratives.* Chicago: Magribine Press, 2011.

Al-Amin, Jamil. *Revolution by the Book: The Rap Is Live.* Beltsville, MD: Writers' Inc., 1993.

Alexander, Amy, ed. *The Farrakhan Factor: African-American Writers on Leadership, Nationhood, and Minister Louis Farrakhan.* New York: Grove Press, 1998.

Alford, Terry. *Prince among Slaves.* 30th anniversary ed. New York: Oxford University Press, 2007.

Ali, Noble Drew. The Holy Koran of the Moorish Science Temple. Scripture, Chicago, 1927.

Ali, Omar H. "Islam and the African Diaspora in the Indian Ocean World." *Black Past.* Accessed August 24, 2016. http://www.blackpast.org/perspectives/islam-and-african-diaspora-indian-ocean-world.

Ali, Syed Mustafa. *Towards an Islamic Decoloniality—Seminar 2 of 3.* Accessed August 24, 2016. https://www.academia.edu/6760988/Towards_an_Islamic_Decoloniality_-_Seminar_2_of_3.

Ali, Zaheer. "Return to Roots: African Americans Return to Islam through Many Paths." *Islamic Horizons Magazine,* July/August 2005, 16–35.

Ali, Zaheer. "Return to Roots: The History of Islam in Black America." *Islamic Horizons Magazine* 34, no. 4 (2005): 17–44.

Ali, Zaheer. "The Message and the Messenger: The Impact of Minister Louis Farrakhan and the Million Man March." *Koinonia* 12 (Spring 2000): 33–42.

Al-Jahiz, Abu Uthman Amr Ibn Bahr. *Book of the Glory of the Black Race.* Translated by Vincent J. Cornell. Galveston, TX: Preston Publishing, 1981.

al-Jahiz, Uthman Amr ibn Bahr. *The book of the glory of the black race = Kitab fakhr as-Sudan ala al-Bidan.* Trans. Vincent J. Cornell. Los Angeles, CA: Preston Publishing, 1991.

Allen, Ernest, Jr. "Identity and Destiny: The Formative Views of the Moorish Science Temple and the Nation of Islam." In *Muslims on the Americanization Path?*, edited by Yvonne Haddad and John Esposito. New York: Oxford University Press, 2000.
Allen, Ernest. "Religious Heterodoxy and Nationalist Tradition: The Continuing Evolution of the Nation of Islam." *Black Scholar: Journal of Black Studies and Research* 26, no. 3–4 (1996): 1–34.
Allen, Ernest. "Satokata Takahashi and the Flowering of Black Messianic Nationalism." *Black Scholar: Journal of Black Studies and Research* 24 (Winter 1994): 23–46. http://www.umass.edu/afroam/downloads/allen.tak.pdf.
al-Qushayri, Abdul-Qasim. *Al-Qushayri's Epistle on Sufism*. Translated by Alexander D. Knysh. Reading: Garnet Publishing, 2007.
Anderson, Mary B., and Marshall Wallace. *Opting Out of War: Strategies to Prevent Violent Conflict*. Boulder, CO: Lynne Rienner, 2012.
An-Na'im, Abdullahi Ahmed. *African Constitutionalism and the Role of Islam*. Philadelphia: University of Pennsylvania Press, 2006.
Ansari, Zafar Ishaq. "WD Muhammad: The Making of a 'Black Muslim' Leader (1933–1961)." *American Journal of Islamic Social Sciences* 2, no. 2 (1985): 248–62.
Austin, Allan D. *African Muslims in Antebellum America: A Sourcebook*. London: Garland, 1984.
Austin, Allan D. *African Muslims in Antebellum America: Transatlantic Stories and Spiritual Struggles*. New York: Routledge, 1997.
Austin, John. "How to Be Black and Muslim in 'Post-Racial' America." *Beacon Broadside*, February 2014. Accessed August 24, 2016. http://www.beaconbroadside.com/broadside/2014/02/how-to-be-black-and-muslim-in-post-racial-america.html.
Aviles, Mary. "Meet the Flourishing Muslim Community in Buenaventura, Colombia." Translated by Eleanor Weekes, Global Voices, November 3, 2015. Accessed August 24, 2016. https://globalvoices.org/2015/11/03/meet-the-flourishing-muslim-community-in-buenaventura-colombia.
Ayoub, Mahmoud. *Redemptive Suffering in Islam: A Study of the Devotional Aspects of Ashura in Twelver Shi'ism*. The Hague: Morton Publishers, 1978.
Aziza, Margari. "The Relevance of Black American Muslim Thought." Blog. Accessed August 24, 2016. http://margariazza.com/2013/03/04/the-relevance-of-bam-thought.
Babou, Cheikh Anta. "Brotherhood Solidarity, Education and Migration: The Role of the Dahiras among the Murid Muslim Community of New York." *African Affairs* 101, no. 403, (2002): 151–70.
Babou, Cheikh Anta. *Fighting the Greater Jihad: Amadu Bamba and the Founding of the Muridiyya of Senegal, 1852–1913*. Athens: Ohio University Press, 2007.
Back, Irit. "From the Colony to the Post-Colony: Sufis and Wahhabists in Senegal and Nigeria." *Canadian Journal of African Studies* 42, no. 2–3 (January 2008): 423–45.
Baer, Hans A. *The Black Spiritual Movement: A Religious Response to Racism*. 2nd ed. Knoxville: University of Tennessee Press, 2001.
Baghoolizadeh, Beeta. "The Afro-Iranian Community: Beyond Haji Firuz Blackface, the Slave Trade, & Bandari Music." Ajam. Accessed August 24, 2016. http://ajammc.com/2012/06/20/the-afro-iranian-community-beyond-haji-firuz-blackface-slavery-bandari-music.
Ball, Charles. *Slavery in the United States: A Narrative of the Life and Adventures of Charles Ball*. New York: John S. Taylor, 1837.
Bang, Anne K. *Islam Sufi Networks in the Western Indian Ocean (c. 1880–1940): Ripples of Reform*. Leiden: Koniklijke Brill, 2014.
Bang, Anne. *Sufis and Scholars of the Sea: Family Networks in East Africa, 1860–1925*. New York: Routledge Curzon, 2004.
Banks, William, Jr. *The Black Muslims: African American Achievers*. Philadelphia: Chelsea House, 1997.
Barcia, Manuel. "West African Islam in Colonial Cuba." *Slavery & Abolition* 35, no. 2 (2014), 292–305.
Bashier, Zakaria. *Sunshine at Madinah*. United Kingdom: Islamic Foundation, 1990.

Bassey, Magnus O. *Malcolm X and African American Self-Consciousness*. Lewistown, NY: Edwin Mellen Press, 2005.

Basu, Helene. "Music and the Formation of Sidi Identity in Western India." *History Workshop Journal* 65, no. 1 (2008): 161–78.

Battuta, Ibn. "Audiences of the Sultan of Mali." In *Documents from the African Past*, edited by Robert O. Collins. Princeton, NJ: Markus Wiener, 2009.

Bayoumi, Moustafa. "East of the Sun (West of the Moon): Islam, the Ahmadis, and African America." *Journal of Asian American Studies* 4, no. 3 (2001): 251–63.

Bazi, Maria Khwaja. "Black Muslim Americans: The Minority within a Minority." *Fair Observer*, February 22, 2016. Accessed August 24, 2016. http://www.fairobserver.com/region/north_america/black-muslim-americans-the-minority-within-a-minority-34590/.

Beckerleg, Susan. "African Bedouin in Palestine." *Asian and African Studies* 6 (2007).

Bell, Diana. "Understanding a 'Broken World': Islam, Ritual, and Climate Change in Mali, West Africa." *Journal for the Study of Religion, Nature, and Culture* 8, no. 3 (2014).

Berg, Herbert. "Early African American Muslim Movements and the Qur'an." *Journal of Qur'anic Studies* 8, no. 1 (2006): 22–37.

Berg, Herbert. *Elijah Muhammad and Islam*. New York: New York University Press, 2009.

Berg, Herbert. "Mythmaking in the African American Muslim Context: The Moorish Science Temple, the Nation of Islam, and the American Society of Muslims." *Journal of the American Academy of Religion* 73, no. 3 (2005): 685–703.

Berns McGown, Rima. *Muslims in the Diaspora: The Somali Communities of London and Toronto*. Toronto: University of Toronto Press, 1999.

Beydoun, Khaled A. "Antebellum Islam." *Howard Law Journal* 58, no. 1 (2014).

"Black, Muslim, American: Interview with Dr. Jamillah Karim." *Islamic Monthly*. February 27, 2013. Accessed August 24, 2016. http://theislamicmonthly.com/black-muslim-american-interview-with-dr-jamillah-karim.

"#BlackMuslimFuture." YouTube video. https://www.youtube.com/watch?v=7Ul3i-AViSs.

Blassingame, John W. *The Slave Community: Plantation Life in the Antebellum South*. Oxford: Oxford University Press, 1979.

Blow, Charles M. "'Black Men, Violence and 'Fierce Urgency.'" *New York Times*, May 5, 2016. Accessed August 24, 2016. https://www.nytimes.com/2016/05/05/opinion/black-men-violence-and-fierce-urgency.html?mcubz=3.

Bluett, Thomas. *Some Memories of the Life of Job, the Son of Solomon, the High Priest of Bonda in Africa*. London: Printed for Richard Ford, at the Angel in the Poultry, 1744.

Blyden, Edward W. *African Life and Customs*. Baltimore: Black Classic Press, 1994.

Blyden, Edward W. "The Call of Providence to the Descendants of Africa in America." In *Negro Social and Political Thought, 1850–1920*, edited by Howard Brotz. New York: Basic Books, 1966.

Blyden, Edward W. *Christianity, Islam and the Negro Race*. Reprint of the 1887 edition. Edinburgh: Edinburgh University Press, 1994.

Blyden, Edward W. *From West Africa to Palestine*. Manchester: John Heywood, 1873.

Blyden, Edward W. *Liberia's Offering*. New York: J. A. Gray, 1862.

Bobboyi, Hamid. "Ajami Literature and the Study of the Sokoto Caliphate." In *The Meanings of Timbuktu*, edited by Shamil Jeppie and Souleymane Bachir Diagne, 123–33. Cape Town: HSRC Press, 2008.

Bontemps, Arna, and Jack Conroy. *They Seek a City*. New York: Doubleday, 1945.

Bowen, Patrick D. "Satti Majid: A Sudanese Founder of American Islam." *Journal of Africana Religions* 1, no. 2 (2013): 194–209.

Bowen, Patrick D. "The Search for 'Islam': African-American Islamic Groups in NYC, 1904–1954." *Muslim World* 102, no. 2 (April 2012): 264–83.

Brenner, Louis. "The Histories of Religion in Africa." *Journal of Religion in Africa* 30, no. 2 (January 2000).

Buggenhagen, Beth A. *Muslim Families in Global Senegal: Money Takes Care of Shame*. Bloomington: Indiana University Press, 2012.

Bujones, Alejandra, Katrin Jaskiewicz, Lauren Linakis, and Michael McGirr. "A Framework for Analyzing Resilience in Fragile and Conflict-Affected Situations." School of Interna-

tional and Public Affairs, Columbia University. Presentation for USAID, Washington, DC, November 23, 2014. Accessed on August 24, 2016. https://sipa.columbia.edu/sites/default/files/USAID%20Final%20Report.pdf.
Butler, Isaac. "Why Is Othello Black?" *Slate*, November 11, 2015. Accessed August 24, 2016. http://www.slate.com/articles/arts/theater/2015/11/why_is_othello_black_understanding_why_shakespeare_made_his_hero_a_moor.html.
Carpenter, Ami C. *Community Resilience to Sectarian Violence in Baghdad*. New York: Springer, 2014.
Casey, Conerly. "'Marginal Muslims': Politics and the Perceptual Bounds of Islamic Authenticity in Northern Nigeria." *Africa Today* 54, no. 3 (Spring 2008): 67–92.
Catlin-Jairazbhoy, Amy. "Sacred Pleasure, Pain and Transformation in African Indian Sidi Sufi Ritual and Performance." *Performing Islam* 1, no. 1 (2012): 73–101.
Catlin-Jairazbhoy, Amy, and Edward A. Alpers, ed. *Sidis and Scholars: Essays on African Indians*. San Diego: Rainbow Publishers, 2004.
Cesari, Jocelyne. *When Islam and Democracy Meet: Muslims in Europe and the United States*. New York: Palgrave Macmillan, 2004.
Chan-Malik, Sylvia. "'Common Cause': On the Black-Immigrant Debate and Constructing the Muslim America." *Journal of Race, Ethnicity, and Religion* 2, no. 8 (May 2011): 1–39.
Chan-Malik, Sylvia. "Profile: Black American Women in the Ahmadiyya Movement of Islam," *Sapelo Square*. Accessed February 29, 2016. https://sapelosquare.com/2016/02/24/profile-black-american-women-in-the-ahmadiyya-movement-of-islam/.
Chan-Malik, Sylvia, moderator. Evelyn Alsultany, Su'ad Abdul Khabeer, and Maryam Kashani, panelists. "A Space for the Spiritual: A Roundtable on Race, Gender, and Islam in the United States." Panel discussion. Accessed August 24, 2016. https://www.academia.edu/6485271/_A_Space_for_the_Spiritual_A_Roundtable_on_Race_Gender_and_Islam_in_the_United_States.
Chappatte, André. "Night Life in Southern Urban Mali: Being a Muslim *Maquisard* in Bougouni." *Journal of the Royal Anthropological Institute* 20, no. 3 (2014): 526–44.
Chatterjee, Partha. *Nationalist Thought and the Colonial World: A Derivative Discourse*. London: Zed Books, 1986.
Clarke, Peter. *West Africa and Islam*. London: Edward Arnold, 1982.
Cochrane, Laura L. *Weaving through Islam in Senegal*. Durham, NC: Carolina Academic Press, 2013.
Colley, Zoe. "'All America Is a Prison': The Nation of Islam and the Politicization of African American Prisoners, 1955–1965." *Journal of American Studies* 48, no. 2 (May 2014): 393–415.
Conyers, James L., Jr., and Abul Pitre, eds. *Africana Islamic Studies*. London: Lexington Books, 2016.
Crook, Ray. "Bilali—the Old Man of Sapelo Island: Between Africa and Georgia." *Wadabagei: A Journal of the Caribbean and Its Diaspora* 10, no. 2 (Spring 2007): 40–55.
Collins, Robert O. "The African Slave Trade to Asia and the Indian Ocean Islands." *African and Asian Studies* 5, no. 3–4 (2006): 325–47.
Crawford, Malachi D. *Black Muslims and the Law: Civil Liberties from Elijah Muhammad to Muhammad Ali*. Lanham, MD: Lexington Books, 2015.
Curtin, Phillip. *The Atlantic Slave Trade: A Census*. Madison: University of Wisconsin Press, 1969.
Curtis, Edward E. IV. "African-American Islamization Reconsidered: Black History Narratives and Muslim Identity." *Journal of American Academy of Religion* 73, no. 3 (2005): 659–84.
Curtis, Edward E. IV. *Black Muslim Religion in the Nation of Islam, 1960–1975*. Chapel Hill: University of North Carolina Press, 2006.
Curtis, Edward E. IV. *The Call of Bilal: Islam in the African Diaspora*. Durham: University of North Carolina Press, 2014.
Curtis, Edward E. IV. "The Ghawarna of Jordan: Race and Religion in the Jordan Valley." *Journal of Islamic Law and Culture* 13, no. 2–3 (2011): 193–209.
Curtis, Edward E. IV. *Islam in Black America: Identity, Liberation, and Difference in African-American Islamic Thought*. Albany: State University of New York Press, 2002.

Curtis, Edward E. IV. *Muslims in America: A Short History*. Oxford: Oxford University Press, 2009.
D'Alisera, JoAnn. *An Imagined Geography: Sierra Leonean Muslims in America*. Philadelphia: University of Pennsylvania Press, 2004.
Dallal, Ahmad. "The Origins and Objectives of Islamic Revivalist Thought, 1750–1850." *Journal of American Oriental Society* 113, no. 3 (1993).
Dannin, Robert. *Black Pilgrimage to Islam*. Oxford: Oxford University Press, 2002.
Daulatzai, Sohail. *Black Star, Crescent Moon: The Muslim International and Black Freedom Struggle beyond America*. Minneapolis: University of Minnesota Press, 2012.
Daulatzai, Sohail. "To the East, Blackwards: Bandung Hopes, Diasporic Dreams, and Black/Muslim Encounters in Sam Greenlee's *Baghdad Blues*." *Souls: A Critical Journal of Black Politics* 8, no. 4 (Fall 2006).
Desplat Patrick, and Terje Ostebo, eds. *Muslim Ethiopia: The Christian Legacy, Identity Politics, and Islamic Reformism*. New York: Palgrave Macmillan, 2013.
Diagne, Souleymane Bachir. "Shaykh al-Hajj Abbass Sall: In Praise of the Tijaniya Order." In *Tales of God's Friends: Islamic Hagiography in Translation*, edited by John Renard. Los Angeles: University of California Press, 2009.
Diouf, Mamadou, and Rendall Steven. "The Senegalese Murid Trade Diaspora and the Making of a Vernacular Cosmopolitanism." *Public Culture* 12, no. 3 (2000): 679–702.
Diouf, Sylviane A. "African Muslims in the Caribbean." *Wadabagei: A Journal of the Caribbean and Its Diaspora* 11, no. 1 (Winter 2008): 83–95.
Diouf, Sylviane A. *Servants of Allah: African Muslims Enslaved in the Americas*. 15th anniversary ed. New York: New York University Press, 2013.
Diwan, ed Maymani (Cairo, 1369/1950).
Donzel, E. van. "Ibn al-Jawzi on Ethiopians in Baghadad," in *The Islamic World from Classical to Modern Times*, A.L. Udovitch, ed. Princeton, NJ: Darwin Press, 1989.
Dubois, W. E. B. *The Souls of Black Folk*. New York: Penguin Books, 1989.
Duderija, Adis. "Literature Review: Identity Construction in the Context of Being a Minority Immigrant Religion: The Case of Western-Born Muslims," *Immigrants and Minorities* 25, no. 2 (2007).
Dumbe, Yunus. "The Salafi Praxis of Constructing Religious Identity in Africa: A Comparative Perspective of the Growth of the Movements in Accra and Cape Town." *Islamic Africa* 2, no. 2 (Winter 2011): 87–116.
Dollar, Cathlene. "An 'African' Tarika in Anatolia: Notes on the Tijaniyya in Early Republican Turkey." *Annual Review of Islam in Africa* 11 (2012): 30–34.
Dwight, Theodore. "Condition and Character of Negroes in Africa." *Methodist Quarterly Review* 46 (January 1864).
Eickelman, D. F. *Knowledge and Power in Morocco: The Education of a Twentieth-Century Notable*. Princeton, NJ: Princeton University Press, 1992.
El Hamel, Chouki. *Black Morocco: A History of Slavery, Race, and Islam*. New York: Cambridge University Press, 2013.
Elmi, Afyare Abdi. *Understanding the Somalia Conflagration: Identity, Political Islam and Peacebuilding*. London: Pluto Press, 2010.
Ernst, Carl, and Bruce Lawrence. *Sufi Martyrs of Love*. New York: Palgrave Macmillan, 2002.
Esposito, John. "Tradition and Modernization in Islam." In *Movements and Issues in World Religions*, edited by Charles Wei-hsun Fu and Gerhard Spiegler. New York: Greenwood Press, 1987.
Essien-Udom, E. U. *Black Nationalism: The Search for an Identity*. Chicago: University of Chicago Press, 1995.
Evanzz, Karl. *The Messenger: The Rise and Fall of Elijah Muhammad*. New York: Vintage Books, 2001.
"Expressions of Islam in Contemporary African American Communities." Fourth Annual Prince Alwaleed Bin Talal Islamic Studies Conference, April 7–8, 2012. http://www.islamicstudies.harvard.edu/expressions-of-islam-in-contemporary-african-american-commu nities/.

Eyre, Banning. Interview with Joseph Braude. In "Feature: Africans in the Arabian (Persian) Gulf." *Hip Deep*, May 2006. Accessed August 24, 2016. http://www.afropop.org/9294/feature-africans-in-the-arabian-persian-gulf.
Fanusie, Fatima. "Fard Muhammad in Historical Context." Video. https://vimeo.com/90333385.
Fatima, Fanusie. "Fard Muhammad." PhD Diss.
Farooq, Mohammad Omar. *Toward Our Reformation: From Legalism to Value-Oriented Islamic Law and Jurisprudence*. Herndon, VA: International Institute of Islamic Thought, 2009.
Fisher, Allan G. B., and Humphrey J. Fisher. *Slavery and Muslim Society in Africa*. London: C. Hurst, 1971.
Gardell, Mattias. *In the Name of Elijah Muhammad: Louis Farrakhan and the Nation of Islam*. Durham, NC: Duke University Press, 1996.
Gardell, Mattias. "The Sun of Islam Will Rise in the West: Minister Farrakhan and the Nation of Islam in the Latter Days." In *Muslim Communities in North America*, edited by Yvonne Yazbeck Haddad and Jane Idleman Smith, 15–50. Albany: State University of New York Press, 1994.
GhaneaBassiri, Kambiz. *A History of Islam in America: From the New World to the New World Order*. New York: Cambridge University Press, 2010.
Gibson, Dawn-Marie. *A History of the Nation of Islam: Race, Islam, and the Quest for Freedom*. Santa Barbara, CA: ABC-CLIO, 2012.
Gibson, Dawn-Marie. "Nation Women's Engagement and Resistance in the *Muhammad Speaks* Newspaper." *Journal of American Studies* 49, no. 1 (February 2015): 1–18.
Gibson, Dawn-Marie, and Jamillah Karim. *Women of the Nation: Between Black Protest and Sunni Islam*. New York: New York University Press, 2014.
Glassman, Jonathon. *War of Words, War of Stones: Racial Thought and Violence in Colonial Zanzibar*. Bloomington: Indiana University Press, 2011.
Goldstein, Joseph. "Tairod Pugh, Ex-U.S. Serviceman, Is Found Guilty of Trying to Aid ISIS." *The New York Times*. March 9, 2016. https://www.nytimes.com/2016/03/10/nyregion/tairod-pugh-ex-us-serviceman-is-found-guilty-of-trying-to-aid-isis.html?mcubz=3.
Gomez, Michael A. "Africans, Culture, and Islam in the Lowcountry." In *African American Life in the Georgia Lowcountry*, edited by Philip Morgan, 103–30. Athens: University of Georgia Press, 2011.
Gomez, Michael A. *Pragmatism in the Age of Jihad: The Precolonial State of Bundu*. New York: Cambridge University Press, 1992.
Gomez, Michael. *Black Crescent: The Experience and Legacy of African Muslims in the Americas*. New York: Cambridge University Press, 2005.
Gomez, Michael. *Reversing Sail: History of the African Diaspora*. New York: Cambridge University Press, 2005.
Griffin, Cyrus. "The Unfortunate Moor." *Natchez Southern Galaxy*, December 13, 1827. Reprinted in *African Muslims in Antebellum America: A Sourcebook*, edited by Allan Austin. London: Garland, 1984.
Habiballa, Leena. "Seeds of Sudanese Identity: Unsettling the Logic of Racialisation." *Qahwa Project*. Accessed August 24, 2016. http://www.qahwaproject.com/archive/2015/11/26/seeds-of-sudanese-identity-unsettling-the-logic-of-racialisation.
Hackett, Rosalind I. J., and Benjamin F. Soares. *New Media and Religious Transformations in Africa*. Bloomington: Indiana University Press, 2014.
Haddad, Yvonne Yazbeck, and John L. Esposito, eds. *Muslims on the Americanization Path?* New York: Oxford University Press, 2000.
Haley, Alex. *Roots*. Garden City, NJ: Doubleday, 1976.
Hall, Bruce. *A History of Race in Muslim West Africa, 1600–1960*. New York: Cambridge University Press, 2011.
Halverson, Jeffrey R. "West African Islam in Colonial and Antebellum South Carolina." *Journal of Muslim Minority Affairs* 36, no. 3 (August 2016).
Hamu, Mahmud. *Al-Kashf an al-makhtutat al-arabiyya wa al-maktubat bil-harf al arabi fi mintaqat al sahil al-Ifriq*. Manuscript. n.d. Timbuktu.

Harun, A. S. M., ed. *Rasa'il al-Jahiz*. Vol. 1. Cairo, 1964.
Hassan, Budour Youssef. "African-Palestinian Community's Deep Roots in Liberation Struggle." *Electronic Intifada*. Accessed August 24, 2016. https://electronicintifada.net/content/african-palestinian-communitys-deep-roots-liberation-struggle/14682.
Hawley, John C., ed. *India in Africa, Africa in India: Indian Ocean Cosmopolitanisms*. Bloomington: Indiana University Press, 2008.
Haykal, Muhammad. *The Life of Muhammad*. Kuala Lumpur: Islamic Book Trust, 1994.
Hiskett, Mervyn. *A History of Hausa Islamic Verse*. London: University of London School of Oriental and African Studies, 1975.
Hunwick, John O. *West Africa, Islam, and the Arab World*. Princeton, NJ: Markus Wiener Publishers, 2006.
Hunwick, John O., and Eve Troutt Powell. *The African Diaspora in the Mediterranean Lands of Islam*. Princeton, NJ: Markus Wiener Publishers, 2001.
Iddrisu, Abdulai. *Contesting Islam in Africa: Homegrown Wahhabism and Muslim Identity in Northern Ghana, 1920–2010*. Durham, NC: Carolina Academic Press, 2013.
Inloes, Amina. "Racial 'Othering' in Shi'i Sacred History: Jawn ibn Huwayy, the 'African Slave,' and the Ethnicities of the Twelve Imams." *Journal of Shi'a Islamic Studies* 7, no. 4 (Autumn 2014): 411–39.
Interview with W.D. Muhammad. Chicago, Illinois, July 25, 1979.
Iwuchukwu, Marinus C. *Muslim-Christian Dialogue in Post-Colonial Northern Nigeria: The Challenges of Inclusive Cultural and Religious Pluralism*. New York: Palgrave Macmillan, 2013.
Iyad, Ahmad. *Al Tasawwuf al Islami*. Cairo, 1970.
Jackson, Sherman. "Imam W.D. Mohammed and the Third Resurrection." *Marc Manley—Imam at Large*, (blog), September 16, 2008. http://www.marcmanley.com/imam-w-d-mohammed-and-the-third-resurrection-by-dr-sherman-jackson/.
Jackson, Sherman A. *Islam and the Blackamerican: Looking toward the Third Resurrection*. Oxford: Oxford University Press, 2005.
Jackson, Sherman. *Islam and the Problem of Black Suffering*. New York: Oxford University Press, 2014.
Jalloh, Alusine, and David E. Skinner, eds. *Islam and Trade in Sierra Leone*. Trenton, NJ: Africa World Press, 1997.
Janson, Marloes. *Islam, Youth, and Modernity in the Gambia: The Tablighi Jama'at*. New York: Cambridge University Press, 2013.
Jasdanwalla, Faaeza. "African Settles on the West Coast of India: The Sidi Elite of Janjira." *African and Asian Studies* 10, no. 1 (2011): 41–58.
Jeffries, Bayyinah S. *A Nation Can Rise No Higher Than Its Women: African American Muslim Women in the Movement for Black Self Determination, 1950–1975*. Lanham, MD: Lexington Books, 2014.
Jennings, James, ed. *Blacks, Latinos and Asians in Urban America: Status and Prospects for Politics and Activism*. London: Praeger, 1994.
Jeppie, Shamil, and Souleymane Bachir Diagne, eds. *The Meanings of Timbuktu*. Cape Town: HSRC Press, 2008. http://www.codesria.org/spip.php?article643.
Johnson, Michelle C. "'The Proof Is on My Palm': Debating Ethnicity, Islam and Ritual in a New African Diaspora." *Journal of Religion in Africa* 36, no. 1 (2006): 50–77.
Kaag, Mayke. "Transnational Elite Formation: The Senegalese Murid Community in Italy." *Journal of Ethnic and Migration Studies* 39, no. 9 (2013): 1425–39.
Kaarsholm, Preben. "Islam, Secularist Government, and State-Civil Society Interaction in Mozambique and South Africa since 1994." *Journal of Eastern African Studies* 9, no. 3 (2015): 468–87.
Kamanzi, Brian, and Idil Isse. *In Konversation: Reflecting on S. Africa, Unravelling Identity, a Somali in the Diaspora*. Podcast audio. Accessed August 24, 2016. https://briankamanzi.wordpress.com/2015/09/24/podcast-inkonversation-in-konversation-reflecting-on-s-africa-unravelling-identity-a-somali-in-the-diaspora-idil-isse.
Kane, Cheikh Hamidou. *Ambiguous Adventures*. New York: Walker and Company, 1962.

Kane, Ousmane Oumar. *Beyond Timbuktu: An Intellectual History of Muslim West Africa.* Cambridge, MA: Harvard University Press, 2016.
Karim, Darnell. "Islamic Studies Materials." Accessed July 24, 2017. http://www.islamicstudiesmaterials.com/profile/.
Karim, Jamillah. "Between Immigrant Islam and Black Liberation: Young Muslims Inherit Global Muslim and African American Legacies." *Muslim World* 95, no. 4 (2005): 497–513.
Karim, Jamillah. "Profile: The Leadership and Legacy of Sister Clara Muhammad." *Sapelo Square.* Accessed August 24, 2016. http://sapelosquare.com/2016/02/01/profile-sister-clara-muhammad.
Karim, Jamillah A. "To Be Black, Female, and Muslim: A Candid Conversation about Race in the American Ummah." *Journal of Muslim Minority Affairs* 26, no. 2 (2006): 225–33.
Karim, Jamillah. "Through Sunni Women's Eyes: Black Feminism and the Nation of Islam." *Souls: A Critical Journal of Black Politics, Culture, and Society* 8, no. 4 (2006): 19–30.
"Keith Ellison and Andre Carson Discuss Donald Trump's Rhetoric on Muslims." C-SPAN.org, May 24, 2016. Accessed August 24, 2016. https://www.c-span.org/video/?410085-1/keith-ellison-andre-carson-discuss-donald-trumps-rhetoric-muslims.
Khan, Adil Hussain. *From Sufism to Ahmadiyya: A Muslim Minority Movement in South Asia.* Bloomington: Indiana University Press, 2015.
Khan, Muqtedar. "The Priority of Politics." *Boston Review* (April/May 2003). http://bostonreview.net/archives/BR28.2/khan.html.
Khan, Zeba. "American Muslims Have a Race Problem." *Al Jazeera*, June 2016. Accessed August 24, 2016. http://america.aljazeera.com/opinions/2015/6/american-muslims-have-a-race-problem.html.
Kobo, Ousman. "The Development of Wahhabi Reforms in Ghana and Burkina Faso, 1960–1990: Elective Affinities between Western-Educated Muslims and Islamic Scholars." *Comparative Studies in Society and History* 51, no. 3 (2009): 502–32.
Kobo, Ousman Murzik. "Shifting Trajectories of Salafi/Ahl-Sunna Reformism in Ghana." *Islamic Africa* 6, no. 1–2 (2015): 60–81.
Kochiyama, Yuri. *The Impact of Malcolm X on Asian-American Politics and Activism.* London: Praeger, 1994.
Kolars, Christine. "Masjid ul-Mutkabir: The Portrait of an African American Orthodox Muslim Community." In *Muslim Communities in North America*, edited by Yvonne Yazbeck Haddad and Jane Idleman Smith. Albany: State University of New York Press, 1994.
Kratli, Graziano, and Ghislaine Lydon, eds. *The Trans-Saharan Book Trade: Manuscript, Arabic Literacy and Intellectual History in Muslim Africa.* Leiden: Koninklijke Brill, 2011.
Kurtzer, Yehuda. *Shuva: The Future of the Jewish Past.* Waltham, MA: Brandeis University Press, 2012.
Landurum, John B. O. *History of Spartanburg Country.* Atlanta: Franklin Printing and Publishing, 1900.
Larson, Kate. *Bound for the Promised Land: Harriet Tubman, Portrait of an American Hero.* New York: One World Press, 2004.
"Latino & Muslim: A Conversation with Minister Abel Muhammad." *Boriqua Chicks.* Accessed August 24, 2016. http://www.boriquachicks.com/2015/08/31/latino-muslim-a-conversation-with-minister-abel-muhammad.
Launay, Robert. *Beyond the Stream: Islam and Society in a West African Town.* Long Grove, IL: Waveland Press, 2004.
Law, Robin, and Paul E. Lovejoy, eds. *The Biography of Mahommah Gardo Baquaqua: His Passage from Slavery to Freedom in Africa and America.* Princeton, NJ: Markus Wiener Publishers, 2003.
Lawrence, Bruce. *The Qur'an: A Biography.* New York: Atlantic Monthly Press, 2006.
Learman, Oliver. *An Introduction to Classical Islamic Philosophy.* New York: Cambridge University Press, 1985.
Lee, Martha F. *The Nation of Islam: An American Millenarian Movement.* Lewiston, NY: Edwin Mellen Press, 1988.
Lee, Victoria J. "The Mosque and Black Islam: Towards an Ethnographic Study of Islam in the Inner City." *Ethnography* 11, no. 1 (March 2010): 145–63.

Leichtman, Mara A. *Shi'i Cosmopolitanisms in Africa: Lebanese Migration and Religious Conversion in Senegal.* Bloomington: Indiana University Press, 2015.
Levtzion, Nehemia. *Ancient Ghana and Mali.* New York: Africana Publishing Company, 1980.
Levtzion, Nehemia, and Randall L. Pouwels, eds. *History of Islam in Africa.* Athens: Ohio University Press, 2000.
Lewis, Bernard. *Race and Slavery in the Middle East: An Historical Enquiry.* New York: Oxford University Press, 1990.
Lincoln, C. Eric. *Black Muslims in America.* 3rd ed. Grand Rapids, MI: B Eerdmans, 1994.
Lincoln, C. Eric. "The Muslim Mission." In *African American Religious Studies: An Interdisciplinary Anthology*, edited by Gayraud S. Wilmore. Durham, NC: Duke University Press, 1989.
"Literacy and Non-formal Education." UNESCO Office, Dakar. Accessed December 29, 2016. http://unesdoc.unesco.org/images/0014/001446/144656e.pdf.
Littlefield, Daniel C. *Rice and Slaves: Ethnicity and the Slave Trade in Colonial South Carolina.* Baton Rouge, LA: LSU Press, 1981.
Loeffler, Reinhold. *Islam in Practice: Religious Beliefs in a Persian Village.* Albany: State University of New York Press, 1988.
Lomax, Louis. *When the Word Is Given.* Westport, CT: Greenwood Press, 1963.
Lovejoy, Paul E. "The Urban Background of Enslaved Muslims in the Americas." *Slavery & Abolition: A Journal of Slave and Post-Slave Studies* 26, no. 3 (2005): 349–76.
MacFarquhar, Neil. "New Translation Prompts Debate on Islamic Verse." *New York Times.* March 25, 2007. Accessed August 24, 2016. www.nytimes.com/2007/03/25/us/25koran.html?mcubz=3.
Makkah. "The Very Serious Function of Racism." Accessed August 24, 2016. http://makkahmeetslife.tumblr.com/post/134204964827/the-very-serious-function-of-racism.
Manning, Patrick. *Slavery and African Life: Occidental, Oriental, and African Slave Trades.* New York: Cambridge University Press, 1990.
Musgrave, Jane. "Lake Park Man Pleads Guilty to Trying to Help ISIS." *Palm Beach Post.* Accessed July 27, 2017. http://www.palmbeachpost.com/news/crime--law/new-lake-park-man-pleads-guilty-trying-help-isis/ZSNaFgWr2pw0K8wMdXgsRO/.
Marable, Manning, and Hishaam Aidi, eds. *Black Routes to Islam.* New York: Palgrave Macmillan, 2009.
Marsh, Clifton E. *From Black Muslims to Muslims: The Transition from Separatism to Islam, 1930–1980.* Metuchen, NJ: Scarecrow Press, 1984.
Marsh, Clifton E. *The Lost-Found Nation of Islam in America.* Lanham, MD: Scarecrow Press, 2000.
Marsh, Clifton. Interview, Imam Wallace D. Muhammad. 1984.
Marsh, Wendell Hassan. "Dehistoricizing Islam in Africa." *Comparative Studies of South Asia, Africa and the Middle East* 35, no. 3 (2015), 656–666.
Martin, B. G. *Muslim Brotherhoods in 19th-Century Africa.* Cambridge: Cambridge University Press, 2003.
Masjid Muhammad, the Nations Mosque. Unpublished manuscript. Washington, DC., 2012.
Interview with Imam WD Muhammad. Chicago, IL. July 25, 1979.
Mattoso, Katia M. de Queiros. *To Be a Slave in Brazil, 1550–1888.* Arthur Goldhammer, trans. New Brunswick and London: Rutgers University Press, 1994.
Mbacke, Amadu Bamba. *Massalik Al-Jinaan.* Rabat: Dar El Kitab, 1984.
Mbacke, Khadim. *Sufism and Religious Brotherhoods in Senegal.* Princeton, NJ: Markus Wiener Publishers, 2005.
McCloud, Aminah. *African American Islam.* New York: Routledge, 1994.
McCloud, Aminah Beverly. "African-American Muslim Intellectual Thought: The Story of Islamophobia." *Souls: A Critical Journal of Black Politics, Culture, and Society* 9, no. 2 (2007): 171–81.
McIntosh, Janet. *The Edge of Islam: Power, Personhood, and Ethnoreligious Boundaries of the Kenya Coast.* Durham, NC: Duke University Press, 2009.
Mirmotahari, Emad. *Islam in the Eastern African Novel.* New York: Palgrave Macmillan, 2011.

Mirzai, Behnaz A. "African Presence in Iran: Identity and Its Reconstruction in the 19th and 20th Centuries." *Revue d'Histoire Outre-Mers* 89, no. 33–37 (2002): 229–46.

Moghe, Sonia, Holly Yan, and Greg Botelho. "Douglas McAuthur McCain: From American Kid to Jihadi in Syria." CNN, September 3, 2014. Accessed July 27, 2017.http://www.cnn.com/2014/08/27/us/who-was-douglas-mccain/index.html.

Mohammed, Imam W. Deen. *Mohammed Speaks*. Chicago: WDM Publications, 1999.

Mohammed, W. Deen. "Youth Dawa Class (Al Fatiha)." Lecture, Chicago, Illinois, October 8, 2001.

Muhammad, Brian E. "A New Imam and a New Day of Unity, Cooperation." *Final Call*, July 8, 2013. Accessed August 24, 2016 http://www.finalcall.com/artman/publish/National_News_2/article_10048.shtml.

Muhammad, Elijah. *Message to the Blackman in America*. United Brothers Communication Systems, 1965.

WD Mohammed Schools of Atlanta. Accessed July 27, 2017. http://mohammedschools.org.

"Mr. Muhammad Answers Critics: Authority from Allah None Other." *Muhammad Speaks*, August 2, 1962. Accessed August 24, 2016.

Muhammad, Fard. "The Supreme Wisdom Lessons." *The Lost Found Nation of Islam in North America*. Accessed on July 27, 2017. https://www.scribd.com/document/10047804/The-Supreme-Wisdom-Lessons.

Muhammad, Hakeem. "Is Kant better than the Qu'ran? A Black Muslim Response." Patheos, April 28, 2016. Accessed August 24, 2016. http://www.pathcos.com/blogs/truthtopower/2016/04/no-kant-is-not-better-than-the-quran-a-black-muslim-response/?ref_widget=gr_trending&ref_blog=grails&ref_post=muslim.

Muhammad, Precious R. "An African Muslim Prince Goes to Boston in 1828." *Muslim History Detective,* February 26, 2014. http://www.patheos.com/blogs/preciousmuhammad/2014/02/an-african-muslim-prince-goes-to-boston-in-1828.

Muhammad, Wallace D. *Al-Islam, Unity and Leadership*. Chicago: Sense Maker, 1991.

Muhammad, Wallace D. *An African American Genesis*. Chicago: Progressions Publishing, 1986.

Muhammad, Wallace D. *As the Light Shineth from the East*. Chicago: WDM Publications, 1980.

Muhammad, Wallace D. *Book of Muslim Names*. Chicago: Honorable Elijah Muhammad Mosque No. 2, 1976.

Muhammad, Wallace D. *Focus on Al-Islam: A Series of Interviews with Imam W. Deen Muhammad in Pittsburgh, Pennsylvania*. Chicago: Zakat Publications, 1988.

Muhammad, Wallace D. *Imam W. Deen Muhammad Speaks from Harlem N.Y.: Challenges That Face Man Today*. Chicago: W.D. Muhammad Publications, 1985.

Muhammad, Wallace D. *Lectures of Emam Muhammad*. Chicago: Zakat Propagation, Fund Publications, 1978.

Muhammad, Wallace D. *The Man and Woman in Islam*. Chicago: Honorable Elijah Muhammad Mosque No. 2, 1976.

Muhammad, Wallace D. *Prayer and al-Islam*. Chicago: Muhammad Islamic Foundation, 1982.

Muhammad, Wallace D. *Ramadan Session*. Homewood, IL, 2003.

Muhammad, Wallace D. *Religion on the Line: Al-Islam, Judaism, Catholicism, Protestantism*. Chicago: W.D. Muhammad Publications, 1983.

Muhammad, Wallace D. *The Teachings of W.D. Muhammad (Elementary Level)*. Chicago: Honorable Elijah Muhammad Mosque No. 2, 1976.

Muhammad, Wallace D. *The Teachings of W.D. Muhammad (Secondary Level)*. Chicago: Honorable Elijah Muhammad Mosque No. 2, 1976.

Muhammad, Warith D. *As the Light Shineth from the East*. WDM Publishing, 1980.

Muhammad, Warith Deen. *Al-Islam: Unity & Leadership*. Chicago: Sense Maker, 1991.

Muhammad, W.D. *Imam W. Deen Muhammad Speaks from Harlem, N.Y.: Challenges That Face Man Today*. Chicago: Zakat Publications, 1988.

Muhammad, W. D. *An African American Genesis*. Chicago: Progressions Publishing, 1986.

Muhammad, W. Deen. "Justice in Islam: How Close Are We Muslims to Western Democracy?" *Muslim Journal*, August 24, 2001.
Na'Allah, Abdul-Rasheed. *African Discourse in Islam, Oral Traditions, and Performance.* New York: Routledge, 2009.
Nash, Michael. *Islam among Urban Blacks: Muslims in Newark, New Jersey: A Social History.* Lanham, MD: University Press of America, 2008.
New America Foundation. Accessed July 28, 2017. https://www.newamerica.org.
Ngom, Fallou. *Muslims beyond the Arab World: The Odyssey of Ajami and the Murriddiya.* New York: Oxford University Press, 2016.
Nkrumah, Kwame. "Flower of Learning." Inaugural address delivered while chancellor at the University of Ghana, November 25, 1961.
Noor, Abdul. *The Supreme Understanding: The Teachings of Islam in North America.* Lincoln, NE: Writers Club Press, 2002.
Nyang, Sulayman. *Islam in the United States of America.* Chicago: Kazi Publications, 1999.
O'Connor, Kathleen M. "The Islamic Jesus: Messiahood and Human Divinity in African American Muslim Exegesis." *Journal of the American Academy of Religion* 66, no. 3 (Autumn 1998): 493–532.
Oded, Arye. *Islam and Politics in Kenya.* Boulder, CO: Lynne Rienner, 2000.
Omanson, Lisa Gail. "African-American and Arab American Muslim Communities in the Detroit Ummah." Master's thesis, University of Iowa, 2013. http://ir.uiowa.edu/etd/2597.
Perez, Michael V., and Fatima Bahloul, eds. "Imam Warith Deen Mohammed: 'If Be Become Independent Thinkers, We Can make a Contribution.'" *Islamica Magazine*, September 11, 2008. Accessed August 24, 2016.http://www.patheos.com/blogs/altmuslim/2008/09/if_we_ become_independent_thinkers_we_can_make_a_contribution/.
Powell, Eve Troutt. *A Different Shade of Colonialism: Egypt, Great Britain, and the Mastery of the Sudan.* Berkeley: University of California Press, 2003.
Pyatt, Sherman, and John Meffert. *Black America Series.* Charleston, SC: Arcadia Publishing, 2000.
Quinn, Charlotte A., and Frederick Quinn. *Pride, Faith, and Fear: Islam in Sub-Saharan Africa.* New York: Oxford University Press, 2003.
Raboteau, Albert J. *Slave Religion: The "Invisible Institution" in the Antebellum South.* Oxford: Oxford University Press, 2004.
Rahemtulla, Shadaab. *Qur'an of the Oppressed: Liberation Theology and Gender Justice in Islam.* New York: Oxford University Press, 2017.
Rahim, Imam Ibrahim A., and Imam Wazir Ali. *The Book of Letters for the Inheritors: An Academic Guide for 21st Century Imams in Support of Imam WD Muhammad.* Unpublished manuscript, 2012.
Rahman, Fazlur. *Islam.* Chicago: University of Chicago Press, 1968.
Rashid, Hussein, and Precious Rasheeda Muhammad. "American Muslim (Un)Exceptionalism: #BlackLivesMatter and #BringBackOurGirls." *Journal of Africana Religions* 3, no. 4 (2015): 478–95.
Rashid, Samory. *Black Muslims in the US.* New York: Palgrave Macmillan, 2013.
Rashid, Samory. "The Islamic Origins of Spanish Florida's Ft. Musa." *Journal of Muslim Minority Affairs* 21, no. 2 (2001): 209–26.
Reddie, Richard. *Black Muslims in Britain.* Oxford: Lion Books, 2009.
Reis, João José. *Slave Rebellion in Brazil: The Muslim Uprising of 1835 in Bahia.* Translated by Arthur Brakel. Baltimore: Johns Hopkins University Press, 1993.
Renne, Elisha P. "The Hijab as a Moral Space in Northern Nigeria." In *African Dress: Fashion, Agency, Performance*, edited by Karen Tranberg Hansen and D. Soyini Madison, 92–110. London: Bloomsbury Academic, 2013.
Riccio, Bruce. "Transnational Mouridism and the Afro-Muslim Critique of Italy." *Journal of Ethnic and Migration Studies* 30, no. 5 (2004): 929–44.
Robinson, David. *Muslim Societies in African History: New Approaches to African History.* Cambridge: Cambridge University Press, 2004.
Roderick, Bradley Price. "A Brief Look at the Roots and Development of the Nation of Islam." Renaissance. Accessed August 24, 2016. http://www.renaissance.com.pk/janrefl99.html.

Rouse, Carolyn, and Janet Hoskins. "Purity, Soul Food, and Sunni Islam: Explorations at the Intersection of Consumption and Resistance." *Cultural Anthropology* 19, no. 2 (2004): 226–49.
Roy, Asim. *The Islamic Syncretist Tradition in Bengal.* Princeton, NJ: Princeton University Press, 1983.
Rupiah, Kiri. "Authentically Black, Authentically Arab: A Roundtable on Afro-Arab Identity." *Afripop!*, February 4, 2016. Accessed August 24, 2016. http://afripopmag.com/2016/02/04/authentically-black-authentically-arab-a-roundtable-on-afro-arab-identity/?utm_content=buffer0ed5c&utm_medium=social&utm_source=twitter.com&utm_campaign=buffer.
Saahir, Michael. *The Honorable Elijah Muhammad: The Man behind the Men.* N.p.: Words Make People Publishing, 2011.
Sager, Dirk. "Communicating for Survival." Interview. Station ZDF, German Television. *World Community of Islam.* News release, December 27, 1979.
Sanneh, Lamin. *Beyond Jihad: The Pacifist Tradition in West African Islam.* New York: Oxford University Press, 2016.
Sanneh, Lamin O. *The Crown and the Turban: Muslims and West African Pluralism.* Boulder, CO: Westview Press, 1997.
Schlee, Gunther, and Abdullahi A. Shongolo. *Islam and Ethnicity in Northern Kenya and Southern Ethiopia.* Woodbridge: James Currey, 2012.
Scheele, Judith. "A Pilgrimage to Arawan: Religious Legitimacy, Status, and Ownership in Timbuktu." *American Ethnologist* 40, no. 1 (2013): 165–81.
Schmidt, Leigh. *Restless Souls. The Making of American Spirituality.* Berkeley: University of California Press, 2005.
Schulz, Dorothea E. *Muslims and New Media in West Africa: Pathways to God.* Bloomington: Indiana University Press, 2011.
Seesemann, Rudiger. *The Divine Flood: Ibrahim Niasse and the Roots of a Twentieth-Century Sufi Revival.* New York: Oxford University Press, 2011.
Segal, Ronald. *Islam's Black Slaves: The Other Black Diaspora.* New York: Farrar, Straus and Giroux, 2001.
Shakur, Amaddou. "Islam in America: The Middle Period (1900–1950)." *Islamic Horizons Magazine*, May/June 2016.
Shikh Ahmad Kuftaro Foundation. Accessed July 23, 2017. http://www.abunour.net/index.php?lan=4.
Sikainga, Ahmad Alawad. *Slaves into Workers: Emancipation and Labor in Colonial Sudan.* Austin: University of Texas Press, 1996.
Simmons, Gwendolyn Zoharah. "From Muslims in America to American Muslims." *Journal of Islamic Law and Culture* 10, no. 3 (2008): 254–80.
Simpson, Diane. "Syncretism in African Cultures." 1995. Reprint, *The University of Western Ontario Journal of Anthropology* 2, no. 1 (2011).
Singleton, Brent D. "African Bibliophiles: Books and Libraries in Medieval Timbuktu." *Libraries and Culture* 39, no. 1 (2004).
Skerry, Peter. "Americas Other Muslims." *Wilson Quarterly*, Autumn 2005. http://archive.wilsonquarterly.com/essays/americas-other-muslims.
Smith, Steven T. "An Historical Account of the American Muslim Mission with Specific Reference to North Carolina." Master's thesis, Southeastern Baptist Theological Seminary, 1984.
Soares, Benjamin. *Islam and the Prayer Economy: History and Authority in a Malian Town.* Edinburgh: Edinburgh University Press, 2005.
Sobczyk, Rita, and Rosa Soriano. "Beyond 'Mouridcentrism': Lived Islam in the Context of Senegalese Migrations." *African Diaspora* 8, no. 2 (2015): 174–99.
Sobel, Mechal. *Traeblin' On: The Slave Journey to an Afro-Baptist Faith.* Westport, CT: Greenwood Press, 1979.
Sounaye, Abdoulaye. "Mobile Sunna: Islam, Small Media and Community in Niger." *Social Compass* 61, no. 1 (March 2014): 21–29.
Spadola, Emilio. *The Calls of Islam: Sufis, Islamists, and Mass Mediation in Urban Morocco.* Bloomington: Indiana University Press, 2014.

Taylor, Ula. "Elijah Muhammad's Nation of Islam: Separatism, Regendering, and a Secular Approach to Black Power after Malcolm X (1965–1975)." In *Freedom North: Black Freedom Struggles Outside the South, 1940–1980*, edited by Jeanne Theoharis and Komozi Woodard, 177–98. New York: Palgrave Macmillan, 2003.

Terrill, Robert E. *The Cambridge Companion to Malcolm X*. Cambridge: Cambridge University Press, 2010.

Terry, Don. "W. Deen Mohammed: A Leap of Faith." *Chicago Tribune*, October 20, 2002.

Thornton, John. *Africa and Africans in the Making of the Atlantic World: 1400–1680*. New York: Cambridge University Press, 1993.

Thurston, Alex. "Muslim Politics and Shari'a in Kano State, Northern Nigeria," *African Affairs*, 114, no. 454 (2015): 28–51.

Tiilikainen, Marja. "Somali Women and Daily Islam in the Diaspora." *Social Compass* 50, no. 1 (2003): 59–69.

Tinaz, Nuri. "Black Islam in Diaspora: The Case of Nation of Islam (NOI) in Britain." *Journal of Muslim Minority Affairs* 26, no. 2 (2006): 151–70.

"Treaty with Morocco June 28 and July 15, 1786." Avalon Project. Accessed February 12, 2017. http://avalon.law.yale.edu/18th_century/bar1786t.asp.

Toynbee, Arnold J. *A Study of History*. Vol. 1. London: Oxford University Press, 1939.

Trimingham, J. Spencer. *The Sufi Orders in Islam*. Oxford: Clarendon Press, 1971.

Turner, L. D. *Africanisms in the Gullah Dialect*. Columbia, SC: University of South Carolina Press, 2002.

Turner, Richard Brent. "African Muslim Slaves and Islam in Antebellum America." *The Cambridge Companion to American Islam*, edited by Juliane Hammer and Omid Safi, 28–34. New York: Cambridge University Press, 2013, 28–44.

Turner, Richard Brent. "Edward Wilmot Blyden and PanAfricanism: The Ideological Roots of Islam and Black Nationalism in the United States." *Muslim World* 87, no. 2 (1997): 169–82.

Turner, Richard Brent. *Islam in the African-American Experience*. Bloomington: Indiana University Press, 2003.

Turner, Richard Brent. "What Shall We Call Him: Islam and African-American Identity." *Journal of Religious Thought* 51, no. 1 (1995): 1–28.

Vahed, Goolam. "Contesting 'Orthodoxy': The Tablighi-Sunni Conflict among South African Muslims in the 1970s and 1980s." *Journal of Muslim Minority Affairs* 23, no. 2 (2003): 313–34.

Van Metre, Lauren. "Peacebuilding and Resilience." U.S. Institute of Peace, 2016.

Varshney, Ashutosh. *Ethnic Conflict and Civic Life: Hindus and Muslims in India*. New Haven, CT: Yale University Press, 2002.

Walid, Dawud. "History Relating to Muslims and 'Blackness.'" YouTube. Accessed August 24, 2016. https://www.youtube.com/watch?v=VTX50_Jjez4&feature=youtu.be&a.

Walker, Dennis. *Islam and the Search for African American Nationhood: Elijah Muhammed, Louis Farrakhan, and the Nation of Islam*. Atlanta: Clarity Press, 2005.

Wallace, Mike. "The Hate That Hate Produced." Office Memo. United States Government Document, July 17, 1959. Accessed July 28, 2017. http://www.columbia.edu/cu/ccbh/mxp/pdf/071659hthp-transcript.pdf.

Walz, Terence, and Kenneth M. Cuno, eds. *Race and Slavery in the Middle East: Histories of Trans-Saharan Africans in 19th-Century Egypt, Sudan, and the Ottoman Mediterranean*. Cairo: Oxford University Press, 2011.

Ware, Rudolph T., III. *The Walking Quran: Islamic Education, Embodied Knowledge, and History in West Africa*. Chapel Hill, NC: University of North Carolina Press, 2014.

Washington, Joseph R. Jr. *Black Religion: The Negro and Christianity in the United States*. Toronto: Reginald Saunders, 1964.

Watanabe, Teresa. "Righting Islam's Image in America." *Los Angeles Times*, May 15, 1999.

Weiner, Leo. *Africa and the Discovery of America*. Philadelphia: Innes and Sons, 1922.

Weiss, Holger. *Social Welfare in Muslim Societies in Africa*. Stockholm: Nordic Africa Institute, 2002.

West, Cynthia S'thembile. "Revisiting Female Activism in the 1960s: The Newark Branch of Nation of Islam." *Black Scholar: Journal of Black Studies and Research* 26, no. 3–4 (1996): 41–48.
White, Anas. "A Black Muslim on #MuslimLivesMatter." Accessed August 24, 2016. http://www.altmuslimah.com/2015/02/a-black-muslim-on-muslimlivesmatter/.
Whitman, Walt. *Democratic Vistas*. London: WJ Gage, 1871.
Wiley, Katherine. "Fashioning People, Crafting Networks: Multiple Meanings in the Mauritanian Veil (Malahfa)." In *African Dress: Fashion, Agency, Performance*, edited by Karen Tranberg Hansen and D. Soyini Madison, 77–91. London: Bloomsbury Academic, 2013.
Williams, Eric. *Capitalism & Slavery*. Chapel Hill: University of North Carolina Press, 1994.
Willis, John Ralph. *Slaves and Slavery in Muslim Africa*. London: Frank Cass, 1985.
Wood, Peter. *Black Majority: Negroes in Colonial South Carolina from 1670 through the Stono Rebellion*. London: WW Norton, 1974.
Wright, Zachary. "The Kashif al Ilbas of Shaykh Ibrahim Niasse: An Analysis of the Text." *Journal of Islamic Africa* 1, no. 1 (2010). http://www.academia.edu/6000096/The_K%C4%81shif_al-Ilb%C4%81s_of_Shaykh_Ibr%C4%81him_Niasse_Analysis_of_the_TextIlb%C4%81s_of_Shaykh_Ibr%C4%81him_Niasse_Analysis_of_the_Text.
Wright, Zachary Valentine. *Living Knowledge in West African Islam: The Sufi Community of Ibrahim Niasse*. Leiden: Brill, 2015.
Yan, Holly. "Texas Attack: What We Know about Elton Simpson and Nadir Soofi." CNN. May 5, 2015. Accessed July 27, 2017. http://www.cnn.com/2015/05/05/us/texas-shooting-gunmen/index.html.
Yuskaev, Timur. "Redeeming the Nation: Redemption Theology in African American Islam." *Studies in Contemporary Islam* 1, no. 1 (1999): 29–61.
Zawawi, Sharifa M. *African Muslim Names: Images and Identities*. Trenton, NJ: Africa World Press, 1998.

Index

Abduh, Muhammad, 31
Abu Bakr (Caliph), 17, 19
Abu Nour Islamic Institute, 82
Adams, John Quincy, 47
Al Afghani, Jamal Al Din, 31
Africa and Africans: Christian colony in, 42; defense of, 21; heritage, 50–51; literacy, 30; and race, 20; spirituality, 43–44. *See also* Islam, African
African American Islam. *See* Black American Islam
African American Religion (Raboteau), 12
African Americans. *See* Black Americans
African-Atlantic Cultures and the South Carolina Lowcountry (Brown), 43
African Colonization Society, 47
Ahmad, Hazrat Ghulam, 54
Ahmadiyya movement, 53–55, 62
Aidarusi, Sayed, 14
Ajami, 14, 29, 30
Al Ajrumiyah, 26
al-Akhaari, Abu Zaid Abdur Rahman, 25
Al-Ashmawiyyah (ar Rifai), 25
Alfiya, 26
Ali (Caliph), 17
Ali, Duse Muhammad, 59
Ali, Noble Drew, 57, 58–59, 59
Allen, Dr. Ernest, 62
Almoravid movement, 22
Al-Qa'ida, xii, 83, 100, 101, 108

America and Americans: citizenship, 74; and freedom, 87; and identity, 2; patriotism, 83, 99; pluralistic society, 104; policy, 105; treaty with Morocco, 58. *See also* African Americans; Islam, American
American Colonization Society, 42, 50
American Muslim Mission, 95
Al-Amin, Imam Jamil Abdullah, 81
ancient civilizations, 20
Anderson, Major David, 46
Anderson, Mary, 99
The Aquarian Gospels of Jesus Christ, 58
Arabian peninsula, 17, 19
Arabic language: and enslaved Africans, 46, 47, 48; instruction in, 24–26; literacy in, 26, 28, 29; memorization of, 24; and Nation of Islam, 76; and prayer, 81; replaced by English terms, 83
Asia, 28
Asmau, Nana, 14
Ayoub, Mahmoud, 95
Al-Azhar University, 79

Baba, Sidiyya, 34
Babou, Cheikh, 33–34, 34
Bagby, Ihsan, 81
al-Baghdadi, Imam Junaid, 25
Bakhtiar, Laleh, 83
Ball, Charles, 45
Bamba, Amadou, 14, 30, 32–34, 36

Bandung Conference, 64
Baquqaqua, Mahommah Gardo, 42
Bayoumi, Moustafa, 2
Bengal, Richard, 26
Beyond Timbuktu (Kane), 14
Bible, 58
Bilali, Salih, 9, 11, 32, 44, 48, 49
Bilalian News. See Muhammad Speaks
Bilalians, 75–76
Bilal Ibn Rabah, 19, 20, 75, 100
Black American Islam: vs. African Islam, 52; and Ahmadiyya movement, 54; vs. Christianity, 50; and culture, 81; development of, 1, 7, 9, 11–13, 14, 51–52; and education, 46; experience of, 92–93; and Gullah/Geechee tradition, 43; and identity, 64; influenced by W.D. Mohammed, 69–70, 83; and Islamic idealism, 58; and Islamic orthodoxy, 54, 55, 93; marginalization of, 3, 52–53, 62, 93; and modern life, 86; and Moorish Science Temple, 57–59; recognized by Gulf Arab states, 80; and recruitment by terrorist organizations, 99, 100; roots of, 80; scholarship on, xii, 12–13, 52–53, 62; status of, 91; Sunni, 81, 82; term, 4; and UNIA, 59–61; written records, 40, 41, 45. *See also* Black Americans; Islam, African; Nation of Islam
Black Americans: and civil rights, 55; conversion to Islam, 54; and depictions of Jesus, 78; empowerment of, 95, 104–105; and identity, 57, 58, 61; independent thinking, 86; and Islam, 2; legacy of, 74; and legacy of slavery, 91; migration of, 55; and Nation of Islam, 61; new theology presented to, 71; preachers, 10; and racism, 53; recruited by terrorist organizations, 100; religious experience of, 95; societal issues, 3, 95; and spirituality, 57; subjugation of, 52, 60–61, 61, 62; upliftment of, 75; and violence, 98. *See also* America and Americans; Black American Islam
The Black Church in the African American Experience (Lincoln), 12

The Black Muslims in America (Lincoln), 12, 53
Black Nationalism (Essien-Udom), 60
"The Blacks in America," 100
Black Star, Crescent Moon (Daulatzai), 64
Blassingame, John, 12
Bliss, Dr. Daniel, 51
Bluett, Thomas, 41, 47
Blyden, Edward Wilmot, 49–51, 52
Brazil, 39
Brodkin, Karen, 2
Brown, H Rap, 81
Brown, Ras Michael, 43

Carpenter, Ami, 98, 99
Carson, Andre, 96
Castro, Fidel, 64
Cesari, Jocelyne, 8
Chan-Malik, Sylvia, 55
Chittick, Dr. William, 27
chivalry, 103
Christian, Dayne Antani, 79
Christians and Christianity: in Africa, 42, 50; and assimilation of enslaved Muslims, 11, 40, 41, 42, 51; inferiority of, 58; influence on Western world, 69; vs. Islam, 50, 51; and Latin language, 29; legacy of, 10; practiced by slaves, 12; and spirituality, 55; and UNIA, 59
Circle Seven Koran (Drew), 58–59
Clark, Warren Christopher, 100
clothing, 76
Columbus, Christopher, 11
Committee to Remove All Racial Images of the Divine (CRAID), 78
Community Resilience to Sectarian Violence in Baghdad (Carpenter), 98, 99
Council of American Islamic Relations, 3, 53
Couper, James Hamilton, 48
Curtis IV, Edward, 13, 51

Daulatzai, Dr. Suhail, 64
Democratic Vistas (Whitman), 55–56
Diallo, Ayyuba Suleiman. *See* Solomon, Job Ben
Dien Bien Phu, 64
Diouf, Sylvianne, 45

discrimination, 18, 34, 35, 41–42
The Divine Flood (Sessemann), 35
Drew, Timothy. *See* Ali, Noble Drew
Dubois, W.E.B., 60–61
Duderija, Dr. Adis, 8
Dwight, Theodore, 46

education, 22–26, 79, 82, 96, 103
Ellison, Keith, 96
Emerson, Ralph Waldo, 55
Ernst, Dr. Carl, 27–28
Essien-Udom, E. U., 4, 60
Ethnic Conflict and Civic Life (Varshney), 98–99
Extremism: increase of, 97, 98; recruitment, 99–100; and resilience, 97; resistance to, xii, 1, 9, 93, 95, 96–97, 104; and Western Islamic thought, 9. *See also* terrorism; violence

"Factors Determining Religious Identity Construction among Western-born Muslims" (Duderija), 8
Fanusie, Dr. Fatima, 4, 7, 13, 26, 54
Fareed, Imam Vernon, 85
Farrakhan, Louis, 77
Final Call, 77
First Islamic Conference of North America, 77
A Framework for Analyzing Resilience in Fragile and Conflict-Affected States, 98
From West Africa to Palestine (Blyden), 51
Fruit of Islam, 103

Gabriel (archangel), 20
Gallaudet, Thomas H., 47
Garvey, Marcus, 54, 57, 59–61
Geechee tradition. *See* Gullah/Geechee communities
Geertz, Clifford, 26
GhaneaBassiri, Kambiz, 4, 41, 42, 52
al Ghazali, Abu Hamid, 31
God, 84
Gomez, Michael, 13
Griffin, Cyrus, 41
Gullah/Geechee communities, 40, 42–44, 48, 49

Haalverson, Jeffrey, 32
hajj, 78, 80
Haley, Alex, 53
Halverson, Dr. Jeffrey, 43, 45
"The Hate that Hate Produced," 92–93
Hiskett, Mervyn, 28–29
History of Hausa Islamic Verses (Hiskett), 28–29
A History of Islam in America (GhaneaBassiri), 41
Holy Koran (Drew), 58–59
Howell, Sally, 4
How Jews Became White Folks (Brodkin), 2
Hubbard, Gregory, 79
Husain, Atiya, 2

ibn al Jawzi, Jamal al-Din Abu'l, 21
Ibn Ashir, 25
Ibn Battuta, 23–24
ibn Musa, Ayyad, 32
Ibn Said, Omar, 41, 43–46
ibn Tifat, Abdullah Muhammad, 22
ibn Yasin, Abdullah, 22
identity: and African Americans, 57, 100; and Americans, 2; construction, 8; ethnic vs. religious, 75–76; importance of, 13; and Islam, 75, 80; and politics, 3; and slavery, 10–11, 12
Ihya Ulum Al Din (al Ghazali), 31
immigration: and free expression, 54; of Muslims, 3, 93; and perception of Islam, 2, 3–4
ISIS, xii, 83, 97, 100
Islam, African: history of, xi, 22–24, 51; and Islamic learning, 24–26; and local cultures, 26, 50, 62; practice of, 22, 26; and revivalism, 31–32, 33; scholarship on, 13–14, 35; Sufism, 9, 28–30. *See also* Africa and Africans; Black American Islam
Islam, American: and activism, 2; arrival of, 1, 40–41; development of, 52, 57–64; and empowerment of African Americans, 75; hajj to Mecca, 80; history of, 9; and immigration, 54; presence of, 11, 53, 63, 69; and Qur'an interpretation, 83. *See also* America and Americans

Islam and Muslims: Ajamization of, 30; and authenticity, 82; as continuum, 52; cultural influence, 57; diversity of, 94; five pillars of, 25; global, 77–78; Hafiz, 46; interpretation of, 4, 82; legalism, 83, 93; localization of, 30; madhabs, 23, 85; origins of, 17, 19; propagation of, 28, 54; and racial identity, 22; as source of idealism, 58; spiritualists, 27; Sunna, 43; Sunni Islam, 70, 75, 81; terminology, 76; and UNIA, 59. *See also* Black American Islam; slavery and Islam; Sufism
Islam and the Blackamerican (Jackson), 13, 81, 94
Islamic Society of North America, 3, 53
Islamic State. *See* ISIS

Jackson, Darren Arness, 101
Jackson, Sherman, 13, 81–82, 94
Jawahir al Ma'ani (Harazim), 35
Jefferson, Thomas, 11
Jesus Christ, 58, 78
Jibril (archangel), 20
jihad, 87, 99–100
Judaism, 83, 84
Al Jundayd, 27

Kaaba, 44
Kaba, Lamine, 42
Kane, Ousmane, 14
Karim, Imam Darnell, 85
Khadijah, 20
Khan, Hazrat Inayat, 58
Khan, Muqtedar, 83
Kingsley, Zephaniah, 49
Kurtzer, Yehuda, 83

languages, 14, 29, 39–40, 43, 83
Lawrence, Dr. Bruce, 10, 28
Lawson, James R., 79
Liberia, 47, 49, 51
The Likening of the Darkness of the Merits of the Blacks and Ethiopians (al Jawzi), 21
Lincoln, C. Eric: and Black American Islam, 53; on "black sacred cosmos," 95; on Elijah Mohammed, 61, 62–63, 64; and enslaved Muslims, 12; on Nation of Islam, 4, 59; on W.D. Mohammed, 79
Living Knowledge in West African Islam (Wright), 13
Loeffler, Reinhold, 93–94
Lotfi, 50
Lumumba, Patrice, 64

madhabs, 23, 85
Mahomet (escaped slave), 45
Malcolm X, 64, 74, 92–93, 100
Malcolm X (Haley), 53
Mali, 23
Malik, Imam, 32
Maliki School, 24–26
Mamiya, Lawrence, 12, 95
Mamout, Yarrow, 11, 44, 47
Manzumah al Qurtubi fil-Ibadat (al-Qurtubi), 25
Marty, Paul, 34
Massalik Al Jinan (Bamba), 34
McCain, Douglas McArthur, 101
Message to the Black Man (Mohammed), 70
Methodist Quarterly Review, 51
military, 86
Misbah al Salik (Muhammad), 25
missions and missionaries, 99
Mohammed (Prophet): biography, 17; cartoon contest, 101; descendants of, 71; as leader of Muslims, 75; life example of, 83, 96; and prayer, 20; on race, 18; and recruitment by terrorist organizations, 100
Mohammed, Bilali, 48–49
Mohammed, Clara, 72
Mohammed, Dr. Akbar, 79
Mohammed, Elijah: arrest of, 72; and Christianity, 58; death, 73; as epitome of hate, 92–93; father of W.D. Mohammed, 70; leadership of Nation of Islam, 7, 61, 62–63, 75, 93; legacy of, 64; letter to Abdel Nasser, 79; and Marcus Garvey, 60; power transferred to W.D. Mohammed, 73; rejection of, 77; on religion and culture, 70; use of Islamic terms, 76
Mohammed, W.D.: on African Americans, 104–105; and Bilal Ibn Rabah, 20;

biography, 70–74; criticism of, 81–82; and development of African American Islam, 14, 54; disagreement with, 13; on empowerment of Black American Muslims, 95; on W. Fard Muhammad, 71; impact of, 8; influence of, 3, 64, 69–70, 83, 96; international relations, 78–80, 82; and Islamic history, 9; and Islamic identity, 75; leadership of Nation of Islam, 70, 73, 74, 94–95; legacy of, 1, 7, 88, 91, 103, 105; on Nation of Islam, 71; as patron saint of American Islam, 87; Qur'an interpretation, 83, 84–85; relationships with Muslim communities, 78; religious and social commentary, 85–87; religious binary, 80; and resilience, 98, 99; and resistance to violence, 101; scholarship on, 10; teaching, 77–78; terminology used by, 83, 83–84. *See also* revivalism
Mohammed Schools of Atlanta, 96
Moorish Science Temple: history of, 57–59; influence on Nation of Islam, 62; interpretation of Islam, 64; as Islamic denomination, 62; and Islamic orthodoxy, 55; origins of, 9, 53
Moors, 34, 41–42, 57
Moors Sundry Act, 58
Morocco, 58
Moslem Sunrise, 54
Mosque Maryam, 77
Muhammad, Abd al Wasif, 25
Muhammad, Imam Sultan, 77
Muhammad, W. Fard, 7, 71–72, 73, 74, 75, 76
Muhammad Speaks, 63, 75, 82
Mukhtasar al-Akhdari (al-Akhaari), 25
Al Muqaddimah al Izziyah (Shadili), 25
Muridiyya, 28, 32–33
Murshid al Mu'in, 35
Al Murshid al Mu'in (Ibn Ashir), 25
Muslim Journal. See Muhammad Speaks
Muslims. *See* Islam and Muslims
Muslims Beyond the Arab World (Ngom), 30
Muslim World League, 78, 93
Muwatta (Malik), 25, 35

Nasr, Dr. Syed Hussein, 27
Nasser, Gamal Abdel, 79
Nation of Islam: assets of, 73; and Bilalians, 75; and Black American religion, 95; dissension within, 76–77; and Egyptian government, 78–80; establishment of community, 72, 93; history of, 61–64; influence on American Muslims, 53; influence on Malcolm X, 64; integrated with mainstream Islam, 69; interpretation of Islam, 64; and Islamic orthodoxy, 55, 71, 73–74, 74, 75, 77; legacy of, 103, 105; and Marcus Garvey, 59; origins of, 9; rebranding, 73, 74, 76; reforms, 75–76, 78, 82, 93; as social reform organization, 13; taken over by W.D. Mohammed, 70, 73. *See also* African American Islam
Native Americans, 11, 41
Nazmu Muqaddimah Ibn Rushd (ar Rafai), 25
New America Foundation, 100
Ngom, Fallou, 30
Niasse, Abdallah, 36
Niasse, Ibrahim, 13, 30, 34–36
Nolen, Alton, 101
Nusayb ibn Rabah, 21
Nyang, Dr. Sulayman, 51, 73–74

Oglethorpe, James, 46–47
Opting Out of War (Wallace and Anderson), 99
Othello (Shakespeare), 42
Owen, General James, 46

Paden, Dr. John, 35
Peale, Charles William, 47
A Peculiar People (Washington), 43
persecution, 19
Pitts, Demetrius Nathaniel, 100
Placides, Alexander, 45
poetry, 21, 33
politics, 3, 96
prayer: and Arabic language, 81; call to, 19, 20; by enslaved Africans, 46; instruction, 20; and Nation of Islam, 76
Professor Fard. *See* Muhammad, W. Fard
Progressions, 104–105

prophecies, 31, 36
Pugh, Tairod, 100

Qadriyya, 28, 32, 33, 43
Qawa'id as-Salah, 25
al Qayrawani, Abu Muhammada Abdullah ibn Abi Zayd, 25
al Qayrawani, Ibn Abi Zayd, 23, 25
Qur'an: and African American Islam, 58, 61; as basis of doctrine, 33; context of, 87; and diversity, 18; interpretation of, 35, 83, 83–85; memorization of, 23, 24, 33, 46, 47; as part of Abrahamic faith, 69; read by Thomas Jefferson, 11; and recruitment by terrorist organizations, 100; rewritten by Drew Ali, 58–59; as source of inspiration, 72, 74, 96, 104; studied by W. D. Mohammed, 72; and Sufism, 43; translation of, 84, 85; verses used as protection, 26; and W.D. Mohammed's religious style, 10
Quraysh, 19
al-Qurtubi, Yahya, 25
al-Qushayri, 27, 45

Raboteau, Albert, 12, 42
race and racism: and discrimination, 17–18, 21–22, 34, 50, 92–93; and recruitment by terrorist organizations, 100; terminology, 20. *See also* African Americans
radicalism. *See* extremism
ar Rafai, Abd ar Rahman, 25
Rahemutulla, Shadaab, 83
Rahman, Abdul, 42
Rahman, Fazlur, 87
Rahman, Ibrahima Abdur, 11, 41, 43, 47
The Raising of the Status of the Ethiopians (al Jawzi), 21
Rassoull, Abass, 73
redemption, 95
Redemptive Suffering in Islam (Ayoub), 95
resilience, 97, 98–99
Restless Souls (Schmidt), 56
Revivalism: and Ahmadiyya movement, 54; and American experience, 87; Christian, 55; as cornerstone to Islamic thought, 36; examples of, 32–36; history of, 31–32; and identity, 13; and Islamic traditions, 83; legacy of, 103; origins of, 7; and pacifism, 30; and Sufism, 33. *See also* Mohammed, W.D.
ar Rifai, Abd al Bari al Ashmawi, 25
Rihla (Ibn Battuta), 23
Ring-Shout rituals, 44
Risala (al Qayrawani), 24, 25, 35, 48
Robinson, David, 26
Roediger, David, 2
Roman Empire, 21
Roy, Asim, 26

El Sadat, Anwar, 79
al Sa'di, Abd al Rahman, 22
Sadiq, Mufti Muhammad, 54
Said, Nicholas, 11
saints and sainthood, 33, 36
Salafism, 100
Sankore University, 24
Sayyid, Omar ibn, 9, 11
Schmidt, Dr. Leigh E., 56
September 11 attacks, 8, 69
Sessemann, Rudiger, 28, 35–36
Shabazz (tribe), 75
Al Shabazz, El Hajj Malik. *See* Malcolm X
Shadili, Abu Hassan Ali ash, 25
Shakespeare, William, 42
Shakir, Imam Zaid, 81
Shifa (ibn Musa), 32
Simpson, Diane, 26
Simpson, Elton, 101
Simpson, James, 47
Skule, Joshua, 97
The Slave Community (Blassingame), 12
Slave Religion (Rabouteau), 12, 42
slavery and Islam: and African Muslim traditions, 40–41; and arrival of Islam in North America, 9; biographies of enslaved Muslims, 46–49; conversion to Christianity, 42, 45; and development of African American Islam, 14, 52, 54; enslavement of African Muslims, 11; experience of, 32; Gullah/Geechee communities, 43; influence on Drew Ali, 58; and Islamic identity, 10–11; and literacy, 46, 48, 49; practicing Muslims, 49; scholarship on, 11–13. *See also* Islam and Muslims

slaves and slavery: and dehumanization, 42; experience of, xii; Gullah/Geechee tradition, 43; legacy of, 91, 98; and preserving cultural traditions, 42–43, 49; and property ownership, 45; and recruitment by terrorist organizations, 100; separation of ethnic groups, 39; slave trade, 39–40, 46
Sobel, Mechal, 39–40
social media, 3
Solomon, Job Ben, 41, 46–47
The Souls of Black Folk (Dubois), 60
Spaulding, Thomas, 48
Speaking Qur'an (Yuskaev), 95
spirituality, 55–56
Starett, Gregory, 4
"A Statement With Regards to the Moorish Prince, Abduhl Rahhaman," 47
A Study of History (Toynbee), 18
The Sublime Qur'an (Bakhtiar), 83
Sudani, Hamu al-Arawani, 29
Sufi Martyrs of Love (Ernst and Lawrence), 28
Sufism: and enslaved Africans, 11; and Gullah/Geechee tradition, 43–44; and hidden religious practice, 9; history of, 26–28; importance of, 27; influence on Drew Ali, 58; interpretation of, 35; rejection of, 31; in West Africa, 28–30, 43–44; and zawiyaas, 44. *See also* Islam and Muslims
Surah al Fatihah, 46
Suwari, Al Hajj Salim, 30, 32
al Suyuti, Jalal al Din, 22
Sy, Malik Uthman, 36
Syncretism: and Ajamization, 30; and early American Islamic movements, 62, 63; and enslaved Africans, 45, 53; and Gullah/Geechee tradition, 43; and Islamization, 26

Taqiyyah, 50
Tarikh al-Fattash (al-Kati), 22
Tarikh al Sudan (The History of the Sudan) (al-Sadi), 22
tasawwuf. *See* Sufism
Teage, Hillary, 51
terrorism, 8, 69, 96, 97, 99–100. *See also* extremism; violence

Thurman, Howard, 10
Tijani, Ahmad, 33, 35
Tijaniyya, 28, 33, 34, 35
Timbuktu, 23, 24
Toynbee, Arnold J., 18
Trump, Donald, 3
Tubman, Harriet, 74
turbans, 32
Turner, Lorenzo Dow, 44
Turner, Richard Brent, 58

Umar (Caliph), 17
Umayyah ibn Khalaf, 19
"Umm al Qura," 14
United States of America. *See* America and Americans
Universal Negro Improvement Association, 62
Universal Negro Improvement Association (UNIA), 54, 59–61
University of Islam, 72
Unto Thee I Grant, 58
Upliftment Society, 73
Uthman (Caliph), 17

Van Metre, Lauren, 97–98, 98, 99
Varshney, Ashutosh, 98–99, 99
Violence: Islam associated with, 69; and Muslim solidarity, 2; prevention of, 96–98; resilience to, 98–99; and revivalism, 31. *See also* extremism; terrorism

The Wages of Whiteness (Roediger), 2
Wahhabism, 31, 54
"Wala and Bara versus American Racism," 100
Wali. *See* Muhammad, W. Fard
The Walking Quran (Ware), 13, 22
Wallace, Marshall, 99
Wallace, Mike, 92, 93
Ware, Rudolph, 13, 22, 26
Washington, Margaret, 43
Weiner, Leo, 41
When Islam and Democracy Meet (Cesari), 8
whiteness, 2, 22
Whitman, Walt, 55–56
wirds, 33, 44

Wood, Peter, 40
World Community of Al-Islam in the West (WCIW). *See* Nation of Islam
Wright, Zachary, 13

X, Malcolm. *See* Malcolm X

Yuskaev, Dr. Timur, 10, 95

al Zawahiri, Ayman, 100
zawiyah, 43
Zaytuna College, 53, 81
zuhd, 27

About the Author

Dr. Muhammad Fraser-Rahim is the executive director, North America for Quilliam International, the world's oldest counter-extremist organization with HQ's in the United Kingdom and offices in Washington, DC where he overseas policy issues centering around rehabilitation, demobilization, and deradicalization against violent extremism. In addition, he is an assistant professor in the Department of Intelligence and Security Studies at The Citadel, the military college of South Carolina, and a visiting assistant professor at Yale University. He is an expert on violent extremism issues both domestically and overseas. Prior to his current role, he served as a senior program officer at the U.S. Institute of Peace where he leads their Horn of Africa Programs and served as an expert on Preventing/Countering Violent Extremism (P/CVE) issues at the institute. Dr. Fraser-Rahim's areas of specialty are on transnational terrorist movements, Counterterrorism/P/CVE issues, Islamic intellectual history, Muslim communities in the West, contemporary theology in the Muslim world, and African Affairs. In addition, Dr. Fraser-Rahim worked for the United States Government for more than a decade for the Department of Homeland Security, Director of National Intelligence, and the National Counterterrorism Center providing strategic advice and executive branch analytical support on countering violent extremism issues to the White House and the National Security Council where he was the author or co-author of Presidential Daily Briefs and strategic assessments on extremist ideology and counter-radicalization. Dr. Fraser-Rahim has conducted research in more than forty countries on the African continent, and has worked and studied throughout the Middle East. He completed advanced level Arabic language certificates at various higher education institutions in the US, West Africa, and the Middle East. He is the author of numerous policy reports, Op-Eds, and several upcoming journal articles and is sought after and has been featured on MSNBC, CNN, Al Arabiyya, Al Jazeera, Fox News, BBC, France 24, and NPR, to name a few. He completed his PhD at Howard University in African Studies with a focus on Islamic Thought, Spirituality, and Modernity issues, and his dissertation was titled, "The Making of American Islam and the Emergence of Western Islamic Intellectual Thought to Counter Violent Extremism: A Case Study of American Muslim Revivalist, Imam W.D. Mohammed (1933-2008)". Finally, he is also a Security Fellow at the Truman National Security Project.

www.ingramcontent.com/pod-product-compliance
Lightning Source LLC
Chambersburg PA
CBHW050909300426
44111CB00010B/1453